HONOLULU & OʻAHU

BONNIE FRIEDMAN

Penguin Random House

Top 10 Honolulu and Oʻahu Highlights

The Top 10 of Everything

CONTENTS

Honolulu and Oʻahu Area by Area

Streetsmart

The information in this DK Eyewitness Top 10 Travel Guide is checked regularly. Every effort has been made to ensure that this book is as up-to-date as possible at the time of going to press. Some details, however, such as telephone numbers, opening hours, prices, gallery hanging arrangements and travel information are liable to change. The publishers cannot accept responsibility for any consequences arising from the use of this book, nor for any material on third party websites, and cannot guarantee that any website address in this book will be a suitable source of travel information. We value the views and suggestions of our readers very highly. Please write to: Publisher, DK Eyewitness Travel Guides, Dorling Kindersley, 80 Strand, London WC2R 0RL, Great Britain, or email travelguides@dk.com

Within each Top 10 list in this book, no hierarchy of quality or popularity is implied. All 10 are, in the editor's opinion, of roughly equal merit.

   Throughout this book, floors are referred to in accordance with American usage; i.e., the "first floor" is at ground level.

Front cover and spine Hanauma Bay, a protected marine life conservation area
Back cover Sunrise at Lanikai Beach
Title page Waikiki Beach and Diamond Head

Welcome to
Honolulu and Oʻahu

Brilliant reef fish patrol turquoise coves. Sandy beaches are shaded by palm trees swaying in the breeze. Inland, waterfalls cascade down from forested volcanic mountain ridges. This is Oʻahu, Hawaii's third-largest island and home to diverse and lively Honolulu. With Eyewitness Top 10 Honolulu and Oʻahu, it's yours to explore.

Settled more than 1,500 years ago by Polynesians, Oʻahu attracted subsequent waves of immigrants from around the world. Most people live in the vicinity of **Honolulu**, a city that reflects its multicultural history through its cuisine. Sip your morning Kona coffee in a Portuguese doughnut shop, eat at a Korean food truck, and choose from Michelin-starred restaurants offering farm-to-table island fare.

Honolulu's star attraction is the iconic **Waikīkī Beach**. Once you've worked on your tan, learn about Oʻahu's history by visiting the **ʻIolani Palace**, the **Bishop Museum**, the **Honolulu Museum of Art**, and World War II battleground **Pearl Harbor**. Farther afield, hike into the crater of the dormant **Diamond Head** volcano, zipline over papaya fields in eastern **Kahuku**, or brave the big waves off the wild **North Shore**. Snorkel in **Hanauma Bay** and spot green sea turtles and manta rays, then see more marine animals at the **Waikīkī Aquarium**. In the evening, enjoy fire dancing at the **Polynesian Cultural Center**. Finally, for a bit of Zen, visit the **Byodo-in Temple**, where wild peacocks wander and guests meditate by the koi-filled ponds.

Whether you're visiting for a weekend or a week, our Top 10 guide brings together the best of everything the island has to offer. It gives you tips throughout, from seeking out what's free to avoiding the crowds, plus eight easy-to-follow itineraries designed to help you visit the key sights in a short space of time. Add inspiring photography and detailed maps, and you've got the essential pocket-sized travel companion. **Enjoy the book, and enjoy Honolulu and Oʻahu.**

Clockwise from top: Koʻolau Mountain Range; King Kamehameha Statue; Diamond Head Crater; Waikīkī Beach; fresh plumeria blossoms; Byodo-in Temple; surfing at Hanauma Bay

Exploring Honolulu and O'ahu

The island of O'ahu is full of impressive sights to see and memorable activities to partake in. The following two-day and seven-day itineraries combine some of the best of these and are arranged to make the most of your time on the island.

Key
— Two-day itinerary
— Seven-day itinerary

Bishop Museum

IWILEI

Libby Manapua Shop

Chinatown

Hawaii State Art Museum

Capitol District

'Iolani Palace

Honolulu Museum of Art

0 km 1
0 miles 1

ALA MOANA

Waikīkī Beach attracts both visitors and locals with its fine white sand.

Two Days in Honolulu and O'ahu

Day ❶
MORNING
Hike the **Manoa Falls Trail** *(see p42).* Afterwards stroll along **Waikīkī Beach** *(see p78).*

AFERNOON
Take the trolley to the **Honolulu Museum of Art** *(see pp24–5),* then walk to '**Iolani Palace** *(see pp18–19)* and take a self-guided tour. Walking northwest, head into the **Capitol District** *(see pp16–17)* and **Chinatown** *(see pp22–3),* and sample some street food from the market stalls.

Day ❷
MORNING
Leave at 6am, bring a picnic, and drive to **Hanauma Bay** at **South Shore** *(see pp28–9)* for snorkeling without the crowds.

AFTERNOON
Eat a plate lunch at the **Rainbow Drive-In** *(see p59)* and hike the **Diamond Head Trail** *(see p46).* For dinner get a take-out from **Me Bar-B-Q** *(see p81)* in Waikīkī and watch the free hula show at **Kūhiō Beach Park** *(see p26).*

Seven Days in Honolulu and O'ahu

Day ❶
Take the trolley to the **Honolulu Museum of Art** *(see pp24–5)* and have lunch at the café. After a self-guided tour of '**Iolani Palace** *(see pp18–19),* go to **Chinatown** and check out the many art galleries *(see pp22–3).* Dine at **The Pig and the Lady** *(see p75) .*

Day ❷
Go to **Hanauma Bay** at **South Shore** *(see pp28–9)* for snorkeling at 7am when the air is cool and the crowds are still sleeping. Have lunch at **Town** *(see p75),* then hike the **Diamond**

'**Iolani Palace** was built in the late 1800s.

[see pp16–17] and visit the **Hawaii State Art Museum** [see p17]. Later, sip poolside cocktails at **Mahina and Sun's** [see p81]. Stay to dine on modern Hawaiian cuisine.

Day ➎

Drive up Pali Hwy, stopping at **Nu'uanu Pali Lookout** [see p69], and head to the **Kāne'ohe District** [see pp30–31] to visit the Byodo-in Temple at the Valley of the Temples Memorial Park. Have lunch at **Haleiwa Joe's** [see p101] in Kāne'ohe, followed by a swim at **Lanikai Beach** [see p49], hailed as one of the best beaches in the world.

Day ➏

Drive to the **North Shore** [see pp82–7] and watch surfers (or whales Nov–Apr) take on the big waves. Have lunch at **Giovanni's Shrimp Truck** [see p87]. Continue on to the **Polynesian Cultural Center** [see pp32–3] and explore some of the island's pretty villages. In the evening, indulge in some fine seafood dining at **Pa'akai** [see p101] at Turtle Bay Resort.

Day ➐

Hike the **Manoa Falls Trail** [see p42], then refuel with a hearty plate lunch at the **Rainbow Drive-In** [see p59]. Shop in the Royal Hawaiian Center and other stores along **Kalākaua Avenue** [see pp26–7], then enjoy a delicious dinner at **Sansei Seafood Restaurant & Sushi Bar** [see p81] in Waikīkī.

Head Trail [see p46]. Enjoy a sunset cocktail at **Duke's Waikīkī** [see p80], a beloved Honolulu watering hole.

Day ➌

Visit **Pearl Harbor** [see pp12–13]. Go early and plan to spend a full morning exploring the site. Drive to the **Ko Olina Beach Park** lagoons [see p48] for swimming. Dine at **Monkeypod Kitchen** [see p95].

Day ➍

Visit the world's largest collection of fine Hawaiian art in the Picture Gallery at **Bishop Museum** [see pp14–15], then stop at **Libby Manapua Shop** [see p59] for a snack. Take the trolley to the **Capitol District**

The Manoa Falls Trail snakes through lush vegetation to reach a waterfall.

Top 10 Honolulu and Oʻahu Highlights

Statue of King Kamehameha in front of ʻIolani Palace, Honolulu

Honolulu and Oʻahu Highlights

Oʻahu's hubs are the city of Honolulu and Waikīkī Beach. Most visitors make Waikīkī their base, venturing out on day trips to see Honolulu's cultural attractions, Pearl Harbor, and other parts of the island. South Shore and Kāneʻohe District are in striking distance of Honolulu, and the Polynesian Cultural Center is an easy day trip from the city, while surfers head for the North Shore.

1 Pearl Harbor
This significant World War II site memorializes the lives lost to Japanese bombings in 1941 and offers a range of tours *(see pp12–13)*.

2 Bishop Museum and Planetarium
This state museum offers a fascinating insight into Hawaiian culture. Its Science Garden represents the unique Hawaiian land divisions called *ahupuaʻa (see pp14–15)*.

3 Capitol District
The State Capitol and the former home of Queen Liliʻuokalani are just some of the attractions of this historic district in Honolulu. *(see pp16–17)*.

4 ʻIolani Palace
Built for King Kalākaua and Queen Kapiʻolani in the 1800s, the palace was later the seat of government. It is open to the public *(see pp18–19)*.

5 Chinatown

This historic 15-block district is home to gift shops, food purveyors, farmers' markets, *lei* stands, art galleries, and eateries *(see pp22–3)*.

Oʻahu

Honolulu Museum of Art 6

Arts of the Islamic and Oriental worlds are well represented in this museum, as well as a further 15,000 works by American and European artists. Polynesian works are displayed, too *(see pp24–5)*.

Kalākaua Avenue 7

Waikīkī's main thoroughfare runs along the ocean up to the crater of Diamond Head. Halfway along the avenue are the "Pink Lady" and the "White Lady" – two landmark hotels *(see pp26–7)*.

South Shore 8

The South Shore of Oʻahu has among its many attractions several popular beaches, walking trails over Koko Head, and an underwater park at Hanauma Bay *(see pp28–9)*.

Kāneʻohe District 9

A stunning region northeast of Honolulu, Kāneʻohe has a scenic coastline, lush gardens, and state parks *(see pp30–31)*.

Polynesian Cultural Center 10

On the north shore of Oʻahu, this center explores the pageantry, cuisines, and traditions of Hawaiʻi, Tahiti, Tonga, and other Pacific islands *(see pp32–3)*.

TOP 10 ⭐ Pearl Harbor

Set in a bay where Hawaiians once harvested clams and oysters (hence the "pearl" connection), the infamous World War II site is still a key military base. The harbor's relics and memorials, which incorporate the resting place of the doomed battleship *Arizona* and final berth of the historic *USS Missouri,* are visited by 1.6 million people each year. A museum of military aviation is also nearby.

① USS Bowfin Park

This park, entryway to the submarine museum, plays host to a display of weaponry, including a deadly looking Poseidon C-3 Missile **(left)** and a Japanese Kaiten human-piloted torpedo.

② Battleship Missouri Memorial

Admission to the *USS Missouri* **(right)** offers a standard guided tour or self-guided audio-tour, while the Heart of the Missouri Tour gives a close-up view of the inner workings of the ship.

③ USS Arizona Visitor Center

Thousands of people pass daily through the center, which is the gateway to the offshore memorial. Arrive early: free, timed tickets for the movie and boat ride are gone by noon on busy days. And even then, expect several hours' wait.

⑤ Deck of Surrender

A bronze floor plaque **(below)** in the deck on the *USS Missouri* marks the spot where a mess table was set up on September 2, 1945 for Japanese ministers to sign the Instrument of Surrender agreement in Tokyo Bay.

④ Historical Film

The 23-minute documentary film shown at the Visitor Center gives viewers a broad outline of the forces that led up to the Pearl Harbor attack and the main events of that fateful day.

NEED TO KNOW

MAP D5

Battleship Missouri Memorial: open 8am–4pm daily (Jun–Aug: to 5pm); $29 adults, $13 children; Heart of the Missouri Tour: $25 adults, $12 children ages 10–12; www.ussmissouri.org

USS Arizona Visitor Center: 1 Arizona Pl; 422 0561; open 7am–5pm; www.nps.gov/usar

USS Bowfin Submarine Museum: 11 Arizona Memorial Dr; open 7am–5pm daily; $15 adults, $7 children ages 4–12, $8 seniors and military; www.bowfin.org

USS Arizona Memorial: open 7am–5pm daily; free; book in advance on www.recreation.gov

■ Pre-book tour tickets online to avoid queues.

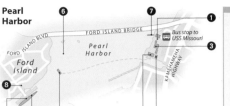

Pearl Harbor

"A DAY THAT WILL LIVE IN INFAMY"

That was how President Roosevelt described December 7, 1941, when Japan made a surprise attack on Pearl Harbor. The bombers crippled US military installations on O'ahu, sinking or severely damaging 18 battleships, destroying or disabling nearly 200 aircraft, and killing 2,390 officers and men. The US officially entered World War II after this event.

8 USS Oklahoma Memorial

Hit by nine torpedoes in the December 7 attack, this battleship sank, and 429 crew were killed. This memorial on Ford Island is near the *USS Missouri*.

6 Battleship Row

The US docked the workhorses of its Pacific fleet along the shore of Ford Island. Vulnerably positioned, the ships sustained the full force of the attack on the morning of December 7, 1941.

7 USS Bowfin Submarine Museum

The *Bowfin* explains how the US responded to the attack. Nicknamed Pearl Harbor Avenger, SS-287 narrates tales of wartime patrols and conditions for submariners (below).

9 USS Arizona Memorial

Floating above the ship that became a tomb, this stark structure is a place to peruse the names of the dead inscribed on the wall (above).

10 USS Arizona Museum

This collection of interpretive exhibits and artifacts is one place to visit during the time you'll inevitably spend waiting for the boat.

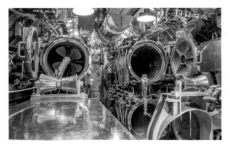

TOP 10 ⭐ Bishop Museum and Planetarium

The State Museum for Natural and Cultural History is a family-friendly center for scientific and cultural experience and study. It also hosts traveling exhibitions and is home to the J. Watumull Planetarium. Almost every weekend, and on many weeknights, there are lectures, workshops, and openings. The museum also has a fascinating interactive science center.

1 Planetarium

The J. Watumull Planetarium **(below)**, was the first such structure built anywhere in Polynesia when it opened in 1961. It has night-viewing sessions, interactive shows, and the "Science on a Sphere" exhibit in the lobby.

2 Hawaiian Hall

The *koa*-paneled Hawaiian Hall, built in Victorian architectural style, is the heart of the museum. Spread over three floors, each one focusing on a Hawaiian "realm," it is home to a collection of Hawaiian and Pacific artifacts. The hall presents a modern interpretation of the island's history and culture via some truly stunning collections.

3 Science Adventure Center

Interactive experiences, including erupting volcanoes and deep ocean exploration, are offered at this state-of-the-art center **(above)**.

4 Hawaiʻi Sports Hall of Fame

This is an unusual installation for a cultural museum, but islanders are crazy about sports, which are a primary form of community-building.

5 Kāhili Room

This collection **(below)** honors Hawaiian royalty through portraits and displays of royal belongings, including the fragile feather standards called *kāhili*.

Bishop Museum and Planetarium

THE AHUPUA'A

Ahupua'a – the small wedge-shaped units of land shown in the Science Garden – were overseen by governors *(konohiki)*, who funneled taxes to royalty. The *ahupua'a* encompassed various farming regions and fishing grounds to meet their inhabitants' subsistence needs.

6 Picture Gallery

Considered the world's finest gathering of 19th-century Hawaiian art, the museum's extraordinary collection of oil paintings, watercolors, rare books, and collectibles is on display here.

7 Library

The extensive library within the complex includes a database of published diaries, narratives, and memoirs, all with an emphasis on Hawaii and Pacific culture.

8 Castle Memorial Building

Dinosaurs, chocolate, robots, spiders, and volcanoes have been the subjects of visiting exhibitions. Most are interactive and aim to attract youngsters.

9 Pacific Hall

This was formerly known as the Polynesian Hall, as it focuses on the lifestyle of people across the Pacific. Artifacts such as the carved figures **(left)**, which give an insight into their rituals, religion, warfare, clothing, music, and dance, are on display here.

10 Joseph M. Long Gallery

This gallery serves as the Bishop Museum's venue for showcasing contemporary Hawaiian art in addition to other items from the collections of the museum, which include Native Hawaiian art pieces and this grass house, or *hale* **(below)**.

NEED TO KNOW

MAP A6 ■ 1525 Bernice St, Honolulu ■ 847 3511 ■ www.bishopmuseum. org

Open 9am–5pm daily

Adm: $22.95, children (ages 4–12) $14.95, seniors $19.95 (discounts for local residents and military)

■ The museum's shop, Pacifica, is one of O'ahu's best gift emporiums. The quality of the souvenirs is excellent, and the wide-ranging book selection runs from archaeology to anthropology, and from history to science.

TOP 10 ⭐ Capitol District

If you had but one day to spend in Honolulu, there's an argument to be made for spending it right here. Concentrated within a few misshapen blocks is a clutch of historic landmarks, a toothsome Asian marketplace, a neighborhood of fragrant *lei* stands, and alluring shops, galleries, and restaurants. And when it's time to sit and contemplate, there's also an ample store of shady mini-parks and cool retreats on hand.

1 Coronation Pavilion

In the grounds of 'Iolani Palace *(see pp18–19)* is a pavilion **(below)**, erected for the 1883 coronation of King Kalākaua and Queen Kapi'olani. The structure, emblazoned with the Hawaiian royal seal, serves as a band-stand for the Royal Hawaiian Band. They perform free concerts at noon most Fridays.

3 Washington Place

This elegant mansion **(above)** has been turned into a museum for Queen Lili'uokalani, the house's most famous resident. It is home to the current governor.

2 Hawaii State Capitol

This airy structure **(below)** is imbued with symbolic references to Hawaii. Pools represent the sea, the columns reach up like trees, and the roofline recalls the volcanoes that formed these islands. At the rear of the building is a statue of Queen Lili'uokalani.

4 Mission Houses Museum

This living history museum includes one of the earliest examples of American domestic architecture, the coral-block Chamberlain House (1830), as well as two other missionary buildings. There is an excellent gift shop.

5 St. Andrew's Cathedral

This Gothic-vaulted cathedral took nearly 100 years to build and is the oldest Episcopal edifice in Hawaii. It was consecrated in 1958, upon completion of the final phase of the building's construction.

6 Kawaiahaʻo Church

"Hawaii's Westminster" **(left)** was built out of 14,000 hand-cut coral blocks. Its name refers to the legend of a sacred chiefess who caused water to flow here, but is also a Biblical reference to "living waters."

KING KAMEHAMEHA

An 18-ft (5.5-m) bronze statue of King Kamehameha I stands in front of Aliʻiōlani Hale. There are four of these statues in existence. The one in the Capitol District was the second commissioned statue as the original was lost at sea near Cape Horn.

Capitol District

10 King Kamehameha Statue

During the King Kamehameha Day celebrations each June *(see p64)*, the King Street statue **(below)** is decorated with exuberant *lei* (floral garlands).

NEED TO KNOW

MAP J2–K3

Mission Houses Museum: 553 S. King St; 447 3910; open 10am–4pm Tue–Sat; $10

Kawaiahaʻo Church: Punchbowl and King Sts; open Mon–Fri

Hawaii State Art Museum: 250 S. Hotel St; 586 0300; open 10am–4pm Tue–Sat; www.sfca. hawaii.gov

Aliʻiōlani Hale: 417 S. King St; open Mon–Fri; 539 4999 (guided tours)

Library: 478 S. King St; 586 3500; open Mon–Sat

■ Re-energize at Café Laniakea (1040 Richards St, 536 7061).

7 Hawaii State Art Museum

Since 2002, this has been home to a collection showcasing solely the work of island artists.

8 Aliʻiōlani Hale

The "House of Heavenly Royalty" is the site of the Hawaii Supreme Court, and it also houses the free Judiciary History Center. Here there are exhibits on Hawaii's legal history and landmark cases.

9 Hawaii State Library

With its colonnaded facade, this building is a cool oasis amid the bustle of downtown. The Pacific section is well worth a visit, as is the courtyard.

KAMEHAMEHA I

TOP 10 ⭐ 'Iolani Palace

A National Historic Landmark, this is the only state residence of royalty in the US. It was built for King David Kalākaua and his queen, Kapi'olani, and was the home of his sister, Queen Lili'uokalani, until her reign ended in 1893. From 1893 to 1968 'Iolani was the seat of the Hawaiian government. Heavily restored, it includes priceless objects and gorgeous decorative touches.

1 Central Hall and Staircase

This capacious and distinctive hall has doors to the front and back for light and ventilation, and is hung with royal portraits. The impressive staircase **(above)** is the work of royal advisor Walter Murray Gibson.

The elegant facade of Honolulu's 'Iolani Palace

2 Blue Room

In this room, the king received guests informally. A portrait of King Louis Philippe of France dominates; the French were among the countries that considered a closer alliance with the Hawaiian kingdom.

3 Throne Room

The king and queen would sit in state and receive their visitors here **(below)**. In 1895, however, in less happy times for the monarchy, Queen Lili'uokalani was put on trial in these grand surroundings.

NEED TO KNOW

MAP J3 ■ Corner of King and Richards Sts, Honolulu ■ 538 1471 (recorded info); 522 0832 (tickets) ■ www.iolanipalace.org

Open 9am–4pm Mon–Sat; shop: 8:30am–4pm Mon–Sat (closed hols)

Adm: gallery self-guided tour $14.75 adults, $6 children; 90-min guided grand tour with film $21.75 adults, $6 children

■ Note that under-5s are not admitted on palace tours.

6 Gates and Coat of Arms

The Kauikeaouli Gate, which opens onto King Street, was the ceremonial entrance, used only on state occasions. Mounted on its bars is the Hawaiian coat of arms **(left)**, which is popular with islanders today in the form of medallions or amulets.

7 Palace Galleries

This vast basement complex, with its chamberlain's offices, servants' quarters, and kitchens, was the heart of the palace. Today, royal treasures are presented here in state-of-the-art displays **(right)**.

8 Sacred Mound

Although most of the royals and chiefs buried here were moved to the Royal Mausoleum in Nu'uanu in 1865, this mound remains an object of respect, as some chiefs may still be buried here.

4 Queen Lili'uokalani's Room

On the second floor is the room where Lili'uokalani was confined for eight months in 1895 after the overthrow of the monarchy in 1893. The leaders of the coup charged the queen with being involved in an insurrection.

5 Dining Room

Formerly the Senate's meeting place, this much-restored room now contains custommade sideboards, a commodious dining table, and an array of portraits depicting European heads of state.

9 King's Suite

Kalākaua slept in a state bedroom with heavy Victorian furnishings, while in the library he conducted business and played cards. One of the islands' first telephones is found here.

THE QUEEN COMPOSER

Lili'uokalani, Hawaii's best-loved queen *(see p16)*, was also a prolific composer. Born Lydia Kamake'eha Paki, and known to her friends as Lili'u, she was an accomplished musician and singer by the age of 15. While her best-known piece is the haunting *Aloha 'Oe*, she composed over 100 songs, many of which she had published.

10 'Iolani Barracks

This diminutive but historic barracks **(below)** now houses the shop, ticket office, and video theater. The shop specializes in designs and patterns inspired by palace ornaments, such as bookmarks based on the carving on the palace door hinges.

🔟 ⭐ Chinatown

The first Chinese immigrants came to Hawaii in 1789, followed in 1852 by large numbers who went to work on the plantations. Upon completing their contracts, many opened eateries and herb shops in downtown Honolulu. After fires in 1886 and 1900, the area fell into decay. Today, after much rejuvenation, Chinatown is once again a thriving community where historic shrines stand next to *lei* stands, herbal-medicine shops, farmers' markets, galleries, and restaurants.

① Merchant Street Historic District

South of Chinatown, this district documents the city's commercial development between the 1850s and 1930s, covering a host of architectural styles. It was added to the National Register of Historic Places in 1973.

③ Open-air markets

Blending Asian and Hawaiian cultures, these vibrant markets **(above)** sell *leis*, traditional clothing, souvenirs, and art. In the morning, stands overflow with fish, meat, noodles, tea, and other delicacies.

④ Honolulu Museum of Art at First Hawaiian Center

This collection of art, in the headquarters of Hawaii's oldest bank, features exhibitions by Hawaiian artists.

⑤ Honolulu Arts District

On Chinatown's eastern edge, this area is home to cultural institutions, performance venues, and events such as the First Friday Gallery Walk (5pm, first Fri of month).

② Izumo Taishakyo Mission

One of the few active Shinto shrines in the US, this wooden structure **(above)** was inspired by Japan's Taisha Machi shrine. The Hiroshima Peace Bell is on view, and on New Year's Day the shrine is the site of local Shintoists' annual *hatsumōde* (celebration).

NEED TO KNOW

Izumo Taishakyo Mission:
MAP H1 ■ 215 N. Kukui St; 538 7778; open 8am–5pm daily

Honolulu Museum of Art at First Hawaiian Center:
MAP J3 ■ 999 Bishop St; 526 0232; open 8:30am–6pm Mon–Fri; www. honolulumuseum.org

Honolulu Arts District:
MAP H2 ■ 1041 Nu'uanu Ave, Suite A; 398 7990

Hawaii Theatre Center:
MAP H2 ■ 1130 Bethel St; 528 0506; www. hawaiitheatre.com

Foster Botanical Gardens:
MAP H1–J1 ■ 50 N. Vineyard Blvd; 522 7066; open 9am–4pm daily; $5, children (6–12) $1

Chinatown Cultural Plaza:
MAP H2 ■ 100 N. Beretania St; 521 4934

■ Tours of Chinatown are available (see *pp46–7*).

Previous pages Byodo-in Temple in the Kāne'ohe District

⑩ Chinatown Cultural Plaza

With an assortment of restaurants and vendors, the Cultural Plaza is a microcosm of Chinatown. Kung fu and lion-dance performances are held here around Chinese New Year.

Chinatown

⑥ Festivals

Chinese New Year is celebrated in traditional style **(above)**, while July 4th and New Year's Eve are marked with fireworks. There are also ukulele contests and Cinco de Mayo parties.

⑧ Hawaii Theatre Center

The "Pride of the Pacific" has hosted an impressive array of films and live performances, from local talent to big names. Allow time to explore the atmospheric interior.

⑦ Dining

Both visitors and Honolulu residents flock to Chinatown to sample the range of Asian food on offer. Vietnamese, Laotian, Chinese, Thai, Japanese, Filipino, Hawaiian, and Korean restaurants line the streets, offering a near endless supply of delicious and inexpensive culinary treats.

⑨ Foster Botanical Gardens

Nearly 100,000 visitors annually pass through these historic grounds **(below)**. Guided tours are perfect for those who are curious about the exotic flowers and trees.

🔟 ⭐ Honolulu Museum of Art

Hawaii's only general art museum, comprising 30 galleries and more than 50,000 works of art was founded in 1927 by the eclectic collector Anna Rice Cooke, whose home had become crammed with more than 4,500 pieces of art. The gracious stucco-and-tile building in the style islanders call "Territorial" was erected on the site of Cooke's original house on Beretania Street.

European and American Galleries ①

This section **(right)** provides a fascinating trip through western art history, with two galleries – Antiquity, and Body and Portraiture – mixing media and eras to reveal how these genres have changed through the centuries.

NEED TO KNOW

MAP M2 ▪ 900 S. Beretania St ▪ 532 8700 ▪ www.honolulu museum.org

Open 10am–4:30pm Tue–Sat, 1–5pm Sun; closed Mon, Jan 1, Jul 4, Thanksgiving, Dec 15

Adm: $20 (discounts for seniors and military, age 18 & under free); free first Wed and third Sun of every month

Shangri La Museum of Islamic Art, Culture and Design: 532 3685 (to book); tours Wed–Sat (book well in advance); closed Sep; $25

▪ The museum's Doris Duke Theatre is one of only two venues on Oʻahu for independent and international films. An acoustically superior and cozy space, it also hosts concerts, lectures, and performances. For details, call 532 8768.

② Shangri La Museum of Islamic Art, Culture and Design

Tours of Doris Duke's 1930s-era seaside mansion at Black Point begin at the museum with a film, followed by a van ride to her home.

③ Arts of the Islamic World

In conjunction with the Doris Duke Foundation for Islamic Art, this gallery is made up primarily of pieces from the foundation's broad-reaching collection – furnishings, beautiful woven objects, decorative pottery, and printed papers. Tours of Shangri La begin here.

④ Arts of Hawaii

This group, which is made up primarily of paintings, graphic arts, decorative arts, and sculpture, includes many of the most recognized images in the islands, such as Theodore Wores' famous 1902 painting, *The Lei Maker* **(below)**.

7 Art of the Pacific, Americas, and Africa

Masks, effigies, figurines, religious artifacts, and other pieces from the Americas, Oceania, and Africa are displayed in separate galleries **(above)** and in periodic special exhibits.

8 Henry R. Luce Gallery

This area of the museum incorporates a large space for changing exhibits, the Hawaiian art collection, workshops, and the museum's offices.

10 Southeast Asian and Indian Collections

A gallery of Indian art, mostly collected by a wealthy Indian family who live in Honolulu, has everything from a carved door to wedding attire. Southeast Asian items range from shrouds to sculpture and ceramics **(left)**. Indonesian pieces appear in both the Asian and Islamic collections.

5 European and American Art

Including over 15,000 pieces, this collection is particularly strong in American works in all media and French 19th- and 20th-century painting, such as the Polynesian themes painted by Gauguin.

6 Textiles Collection

Only a fraction of the museum's immense textile collection is on display at any one time. While the focus is on Asia, there are also fine examples of Pacific *tapa* cloth, Japanese *kabuki* costumes, an emperor's *jifu* (robe), and saris.

9 Asian Art Collection

A centerpiece of the museum's Asian holdings is the collection of *ukiyo-e* paintings, which includes *The Great Wave* **(below)**, part of Hokusai's *Thirty-six Views of Mount Fuji*. The collection is also strong in Japanese scrolls and Ming Dynasty paintings.

🔟⭐ Kalākaua Avenue

Waikīkī's 2-mile- (3-km-) long oceanfront avenue, running from Ala Wai Bridge to the magnificent Diamond Head, epitomizes the dream of Hawaii – gentle surf and vibrant nightlife. Named for Hawaii's playful last king, the street is lined with storied hotels, restaurants, a wide variety of high-end shops, parks, and a host of attractions. It also has seating areas, palm trees, and a waterfall that's a favorite "photo op" spot.

② Royal Hawaiian Hotel

The "Pink Lady" **(left)** retains her cache. Even if you're not staying at this most famous of Waikīkī hotels *(see p116)*, you can take afternoon tea on the veranda or visit the famed Mai Tai Bar *(see p74)*.

③ Kūhiō Beach Hula Show

Grab a spot on the grass or on the sand in front of the large banyan tree and watch *hālau hula* (dance troupes) and performers sway to the charming sounds of Hawaiian music at this free outdoor event.

NEED TO KNOW

MAP G5–M7

Kūhiō Beach Hula Show: Kalākaua Ave, 843 8002; 6:30pm Tue, Thu, Sat (6pm Nov–Jan); www. waikikiimprovement.com

Honolulu Zoo: 151 Kapahulu Ave; 971 7171; open 9am– 4:30pm daily; $14 ($6 children 3–12); www.honoluluzoo.org

Waikīkī Aquarium: 2777 Kalākaua Ave; 923 9741; open 9am–4:30pm daily; $12 ($5 children 4–12); www.waquarium.org

■ You can picnic on the grass at Kapiʻolani Park.

① Sheraton Moana Surfrider Hotel

The porticoed "White Lady" *(see p116)* dates back to 1901. The Sunday champagne brunch is legendary; an evening at the Beach Bar a must.

Kalākaua Avenue

HOW TO "GO DIAMOND HEAD"

The extinct Diamond Head volcano crater is such an important icon that Oahuans tell direction by it – "Go Diamond Head" means "Go east" to locals. Want to sound like a local? Call it "Kaimana Hila" (KYE-mah-na HEE-la), which literally translates as "Diamond Hill." It's also the name of a popular hula.

4 Honolulu Zoo

This compact zoo has a number of warm habitats *(see p45)*. Check out the Komodo dragon. You can also take a backstage zoo-keeper tour or go on a moon-light walk, or an overnight campout.

5 Kapiʻolani Park

This 170-acre (69-ha) park was dedicated by King Kalākaua in 1877. It was a military encampment in World War II, but today it is a place for families, music, and festivals **(above)**.

6 Waikīkī Beach

A lively gathering place, Waikīkī Beach brims with beachboys giving surf lessons; old-timers playing checkers; canoe teams practicing; and locals mingling with tourists in the waves. The whole beach is open to the public **(above)**, including the areas directly in front of the Royal and Moana hotels *(see p49)*.

7 Duke Kahanamoku

At Kūhiō Beach, the figure hung with *lei* **(right)** is Duke Paʻoa Kahanamoku, a pioneer surfer and "Ambassador of Aloha" in the 1960s.

8 Royal Hawaiian Center

This upscale shopping center offers cultural programs such as *lei*-making and hula lessons.

9 Waikīkī Aquarium

Popular with youngsters for its sharks and Hawaiian monk seals, the aquarium is also involved in conservation projects, and hosts reef walks and excursions.

10 Diamond Head

The crater at the end of Kalākaua Avenue **(below)** is two-thirds of a mile across; its brow is 761 ft (232 m) high, and its summit circumference is 2 miles (3.2 km). Take the lovely 0.8-mile (1.2-km) trail to its top to enjoy sweeping views *(see p42)*.

TOP 10 ⭐ South Shore

O'ahu's South Shore changes rapidly from suburb to barely touched landscapes of azure bays, botanical gardens, and a shoreline from which whales can be seen in the winter surf. Though close to the city's action, the coast has almost no services – no stores and few restrooms. An occasional lunchwagon at Sandy Beach and a snack stand at Hanauma Bay provide respite.

5 Sandy Beach

Locals love this beach, and on weekends it's busy with body and boogie boarders. Be aware that waves slam into the sloping sand beach with great force, so extra care should be taken.

1 Hanauma Bay Nature Preserve

Drifting aquatic plantlife, delicate coral, vibrant fish **(above)**, green sea turtles, and rays can be seen in Hanauma Bay. Visitors can learn about the area's dangers and ecological fragility.

2 Hanauma Bay Beach

A visit to this beautiful, palm-shaded beach **(below)** is worthwhile only if you also plan to experience the underwater park.

3 Koko Head Trail

This trail involves a ramble along a steep paved road, followed by a scramble along the spine of Koko Head, and then a downhill path for views of the shoreline and the sea *(see p43)*.

4 Wawāmalu and Kaloko

These two beaches are fine for shoreline pleasures, such as sunbathing or flying a kite, but don't even think about taking on the killing shore break and swift currents.

Kalama Valley

Hawaii Kai

KALANIANAOLE HIGHWAY

72

Koko Head

South Shore

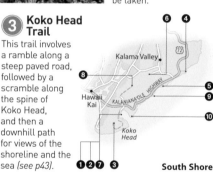

6 Koko Crater Botanical Garden

The scent of plumeria flowers (also known as frangipani) is the lasting impression to take away from this dry-land garden **(above)** right inside Koko Crater.

7 Hanauma Bay Underwater Park

From experienced divers to novice snorkelers and waders, everyone can enjoy this extraordinary preserve. The central area of the park is the safest; strong currents exist three quarters of the way to either side, ready to surprise non-attentive snorkelers.

8 Koko Crater Trail

Buffeted by wind and strewn with rocks, this exposed trail to the crater is one you should approach with caution, good shoes, and a hat.

9 Hālona Blow Hole

This lava tube **(right)** sucks up water from below, then sends it shooting up *(see p43)*. You can climb down close to the blow hole, but it is very dangerous to go near the opening.

KOKO HEAD

The peninsula defining Hanauma Bay is formed out of two volcanic landmarks: Koko Crater and the peak at Koko Head. Koko was the traditional name of a canoe landing at the Wai'alae side of Koko Head. The crater is also called Kohelepelepe. Today, the area is part of a regional park.

10 Toilet Bowl

This rocky pool is known for its exciting churning action as waves wash in and out. People love to bob up and down in the maelstrom, but be warned: there have been injuries.

NEED TO KNOW
MAP F5–6

Hanauma Bay Nature Preserve: 396 4229; open 6am–7pm Wed–Mon; $7.50 ($1 to park); go early or after 2pm

Koko Head Trail: the access road is just to the right of the Hanauma Bay entrance

Koko Crater Botanical Garden: 7491 Kokonani St, access via Kealahou St, off Kalaniana'ole Hwy; 522 7066 (for guided hikes); open dawn to dusk daily

Koko Crater Trail: leave your vehicle at the Hālona Blow Hole parking lot, then walk back along Kalaniana'ole Hwy until you see the trail angle off through the Job Corps Training Center property.

■ For a day on the sunny South Shore, be sure to pack a cooler of ice, water, drinks, and snacks. In addition, it is wise to bring sunscreen, hats, and sturdy shoes. You can rent or buy snorkeling gear for Hanauma Bay.

TOP 10 ⭐ Kāneʻohe District

The area loosely known as Kāneʻohe is within commuting distance of Honolulu but feels a world away – a gateway to the North Shore and its country-style life. Many Native Hawaiians live here, and the area is peppered with historic sites. You notice the difference at once – more pickup trucks, parked vehicles selling fresh fish and Hawaiian foods, and a slower pace.

1 Hoʻomaluhia Botanical Garden

The 400 fragrant acres (162 ha) of this park also function as the area's flood-control facility. The botanical garden takes in themed plantings, trails, campsites, a visitor center, and a lake.

3 Kahaluʻu Fishpond

This is one of a handful of working ponds that date from a time when traditional Hawaiians farmed fish using rock walls fitted with *mākaha* (slatted gates) that let fingerlings out but denied escape to larger fish.

4 Haʻikū Gardens

Planted by an Englishman, this park has a small lake, groves of ginger and bamboo, a well-kept lawn, a gazebo, and a pavilion. It is also a popular venue for wedding ceremonies.

2 Mokoliʻi (Chinaman's Hat)

Visible from Heʻeia to Kualoa, this lopsided conical island **(above)** is often visited by kayakers. It is said to be the remains of a giant *moʻo* (lizard god).

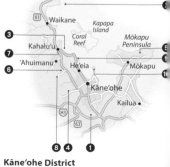

Kāneʻohe District

7 Kahaluʻu

Bordering Waiheʻe Stream, Kahaluʻu Regional Park offers activities such as ballfields, a swimming pool and gym, a beach park, boat launch, and canoe house. It's also known for its turtles **(left)**.

8 Byodo-in Temple

At the rear of the memorial park, this otherworldly structure **(left)** is worth the park admission alone. It's a scale replica of the 900-year-old temple at Uji in Japan, watched over by an immense incense-wreathed Buddha. Enjoy feeding the swans and banging the deep-toned gong.

9 Heʻeia State Park

Perched on a hillside, this is an interpretive park that hosts a number of educational activities aimed at explaining the area's use as both an aquaculture center and a sacred site where spirits enter the afterlife.

5 Mōkapu Peninsula

Visible throughout the district, this peninsula is, alas, out of bounds because it is home to a military base. Despite the hum of aircraft, it is a beautiful sight.

6 Valley of the Temples Memorial Park

This may be a cemetery but it is also a place to take in the islands' cultural diversity and the beauty of the Koʻolau mountains **(below)**. It's common to see families picnicking near the graves of their loved ones; the graves of Buddhists are equipped with food and incense to honor the spirits.

MARINE CORPS BASE HAWAII

Kāneʻohe Bay is home to more than 10,000 US Navy and Marine Corps personnel. The base's location makes it ideal for deployment to the Far East. Historically, this place – Moku-kapu to ancient Hawaiians was called "sacred district" because Kamehameha I met his chiefs here.

10 Moku O Loʻe (Coconut Island)

This islet has a varied history and is now the site of a biological research facility, famous for its study of marine life, especially coral.

NEED TO KNOW

MAP E4

Hoʻomaluhia Botanical Garden: 45–680 Luluku Rd; 233 7323; open 9am–4pm daily; guided walks 10am Sat & 1pm Sun

Haʻikū Gardens: 46–336 Haʻikū Rd; 247 0605; www.haikugardens.com

Byodo-in Temple: 47–200 Kahekili Hwy; open 9am–5pm daily; $5 ($4 seniors, $2 children 2–12)

Heʻeia State Park: 46–465 Kamehameha Hwy; 247 3156

■ The three most direct routes to Kāneʻohe from town offer great views. Pali Hwy (H61) has a lookout. Likelike Hwy (H63) is the quickest route, with spectacular scenery as you emerge from the tunnel. From H3, the entire area is laid out ahead.

🔟⭐ Polynesian Cultural Center

Covering 42 acres (17 ha) on O'ahu's scenic north shore, the Polynesian Cultural Center provides an unparalleled opportunity to experience seven Pacific Island nations in one place on a single day. Though kitsch in places, the center has been immensely popular since the 1970s, with around one million guests annually.

1 Tongan Village
The only remaining kingdom in the Pacific, Tonga has been ruled by the Tupou family since 950. The Tongan Village features drumming, tapa cloth-making **(above)**, and a nose flute demonstration. Visitors can also try spear-throwing on the village green.

THE MORMON CONNECTION

This Mormon center was established in 1963 by the Mormon Church of Jesus Christ of Latter-Day Saints – there is a fairly high Mormon demographic in Hawaii. The center's mission is twofold: to help preserve the cultural heritage of Polynesia and to provide jobs and scholarships for students at Brigham Young University. The school's Hawaii campus is located next door.

2 Tahitian Village
A French territory since 1842, Tahiti is known for, among other things, its fast, hip-shaking dance, the *tamure*. You can learn the dance at the village **(below)**, but if your hips aren't up to it, you can opt for the coconut bread-making instead.

3 Samoan Village
Robert Louis Stevenson, known in Samoa as Tusitala (storyteller), loved the people so much that he lived out his days on Western Samoa. You can find out how to climb coconut trees and open coconut husks at the Samoan village.

Polynesian Cultural Center

NEED TO KNOW

MAP D1 ▪ 55–370 Kamehameha Hwy, Lā'ie ▪ 293 3333 (reservation system) ▪ www.polynesia.com

Open 12:30–9pm Mon–Sat; cultural villages close at 6:30pm

Adm: adult $49.95, child $39.95; show package (includes dinner): adult $69.95, child $54.95; dining & transportation packages also available

▪ **Visitors should arrive before 1:30pm for an optimum experience of the entire center.**

6 Rainbows of Paradise

Every day at 2:30pm, the quiet lagoons come alive as dozens of Polynesians in traditional costume present an interpretation of 5,000 years of Pacific Island cultural lore in a rousing pageant **(left)**.

7 Marquesan Exhibit

Made famous by the 19th-century French artist Paul Gauguin, who spent the last years of his life in the Marquesas, the culture of these islands is represented at the center through weaving and carving, tattoos, and Marquesan songs and dance.

8 Hawaiian Village

There is nothing more representative of Hawaiian culture than hula. This is the place to try the dance for yourself and learn about the symbolism of the moves. At the Hawaiian village, it is also possible to play local versions of bowling and checkers.

10 Fijian Village

The archipelago of Fiji represents a crosscultural mix of Polynesia and Melanesia. The center's Fijian Village features a tribal meeting house **(below)** and an outrigger canoe, while the House of the Gods is the landmark for the whole center.

4 Aotearoa

Wall carvings conveying ancient stories about these great navigators are on display here, and you can also learn about the fierce-looking Maori facial tattoos and watch the famous *haka* war dance.

5 IMAX Theater

The center's IMAX theater features afternoon showings of Hawaiian Experience, a 4-D cinematic extravaganza that puts visitors up close with an erupting volcano, ocean waves, and the full scope of the beauty of the island.

9 Hā: Breath of Life and the Ali'i Lū'au

The former is a lively Polynesian song and dance revue, featuring more than 100 performers; the latter a feast of traditional foods and contemporary entertainment. Both take place in the Pacific Theater.

The Top 10 of Everything

Vegetation-covered peaks in Hau'ula Forest Reserve, part of the Ko'olau Mountain Range

TOP10 Moments in History

1 Formation of the Islands

Each of the islands in the Hawaiian archipelago is actually the top of an underwater volcano. The oldest of the eight major islands (formed some 70 million years ago) is Kaua'i; the youngest Hawai'i, where the active Kīlauea volcano adds more landmass daily. A new island, Lō'ihi, is forming far below the ocean's surface, southeast of Hawaii.

2 Polynesian Migration

Scholars believe that Marquesan voyagers first came to Hawaii as early as the 4th century, with Tahitians arriving later, in the 13th. It was these two great waves of migration by skilled Polynesian seafarers that first populated the Hawaiian islands.

3 Western Contact

The landing of British explorer Captain James Cook at Kealakekua Bay on the island of Hawai'i in 1778 is generally acknowledged to be the first time Hawaiians had contact with Europeans. There is evidence that Spanish ships sailed into island waters in the 16th century, but there are no records of any contact being made with the islanders.

Statue of King Kamehameha

4 King Kamehameha I Unites the Islands

An accomplished warrior chief from the island of Hawai'i, Kamehameha I waged war to conquer O'ahu and Maui, then forced the island of Kaua'i to cede to his dominion. Thus the islands were unified into the Kingdom of Hawaii in 1809.

5 Missionaries Arrive

March 30, 1820 is a historic (some would say notorious) date for the islands. This is when the first American missionaries arrived in Hawaii. The first group was made up of New England Congregationalists, and they landed at Kailua on O'ahu. Over the next 20 years, many more groups of Christian missionaries would follow, taking up residence on all the major islands.

6 The Plantation Era

Beginning in the mid-1800s, the American businessmen who first set up sugarcane production on the Hawaiian islands started importing contract laborers to work the plantations. Workers from China were followed by Portuguese, Japanese, Latin American, Korean, and Filipino immigrants. The immigration of those groups led to the very diverse ethnic mix found in the islands today.

James Cook and indigenous people

7 The Overthrow of the Hawaiian Monarchy

On January 17, 1893, Hawaii's last queen, Lili'uokalani, was removed from her throne and placed under house arrest in 'Iolani Palace. The coup was the work of American businessmen based in Hawaii, though it was not supported by US President Grover Cleveland, a Democrat. He was unable to persuade the provisional government, led by Republican Sanford P. Dole, to restore the monarchy.

8 Pearl Harbor Attacked

It was a quiet Sunday morning when Japanese warplanes attacked the US fleet at Pearl Harbor. This attack on December 7, 1941 marked the official entry of the United States into World War II *(see pp12–13)*.

Ships burning at Pearl Harbor, 1941

9 Tourism

Tourists arrived first by ship and then by plane, and by the late 1950s they were visiting in increasing numbers, seeking the warmth of Hawaii, a place within easy reach of the West Coast of the US mainland. Today, the islands host over seven million visitors each year, arriving from every corner of the globe.

10 Statehood

Hawaii became the 50th state in the Union on August 21, 1959. William F. Quinn and James K. Kealoha were sworn in as the new state's first elected governor and lieutenant governor. The occasion is marked each year by a state holiday, Admission Day (third Friday in August).

INFLUENTIAL LEADERS

1 King Kamehameha I (1758–1819)
The *ali'i* (chief) who in 1809 united the islands into the Kingdom of Hawaii, after defeating Maui's *ali'i*, Kahekili.

2 James Campbell (1826–1900)
The estate of this early sugar baron who died in 1900 is valued at over $2 billion.

3 Bernice Pauahi Bishop (1831–1884)
The name of the great granddaughter of Kamehameha I lives on in the Bishop Museum.

4 King David Kalākaua (1836–1891)
Affectionately known as the Merrie Monarch, David Kalākaua became king in 1874 and is credited with the revival of hula.

5 Queen Lili'uokalani (1838–1917)
Hawaii's last and one of its most beloved monarchs *(see p19)*. Her government was overthrown in 1893.

6 Loren Thurston (1858–1931)
A businessman from the mainland US, Loren Thurston was leader of the 1887 "Bayonet Revolution", which ended the monarchy in Hawaii.

7 John Burns (1909–1975)
A statehood advocate, John Burns was elected in 1962 to his first of three terms as governor of the State of Hawaii.

8 Daniel Inouye (1924–2012)
Hawaii's first Congressman was elected to the Senate in 1962 and served nine consecutive terms.

9 John Waihe'e (b.1946)
The first governor of Hawaiian ancestry led the state from 1986 to 1994.

10 Nainoa Thompson (b.1953)
President of the Polynesian Voyaging Society, Nainoa Thompson has revived traditional voyaging arts.

Senator Daniel Inouye

Music and Dance Styles

1 Hula 'Auana

When the practice of hula was revived during the reign of the Merrie Monarch, King David Kalākaua, a new dance style took center stage. Known as *hula 'auana* (modern hula), it is accompanied by instruments such as the ukulele, guitar, standing bass, and singing voices. It is more flowing in style than *hula kahiko*, and dancers generally wear western clothes.

2 Traditional Hawaiian Chant

As an oral tradition, Hawaiian stories and family histories were related through chant *(oli)*. Ranging greatly in style, *oli* are used for many reasons, from prayers and lamentations to requests for permission to gather flora.

3 Hula Kahiko

In this famous art form, hula dancers are accompanied by percussive instruments made from natural materials and the intonations of one or more chanters. Ancient hula began, it is believed, as a male preserve and as religious ritual.

Hula dancers on Makapu'u Beach

Lion dancers at Chinese New Year

4 O-Bon

O-Bon, a traditional Japanese religious observance, has now evolved into a more secular event. O-Bon dances honor deceased ancestors and are joyous occasions marked by drums, music, dances, and, nowadays, festival foods and fun activities.

5 Lion Dance

The Lion Dance is performed all over Hawaii during February's Chinese New Year celebrations. Acrobatic dancers don a lion costume and perform a dance to a steady – and very loud – drumbeat, designed to ward off evil and spread good fortune. Spectators fill red and gold envelopes with dollar bills and feed them to the lion to ensure future prosperity.

6 The Sweet Leilani Era

From 1900 to the early 1940s, US mainland composers were greatly influenced by Hawaii, mostly as a result of the way the islands were portrayed by Hollywood. This era – when songs like *Sweet Leilani*, *Yacka Hula Hickey Dula*, and *My Honolulu Lady* were written – is called the *Hapa-Haole* or Sweet Leilani era.

7 Contemporary Hawaiian Music

The renaissance of the Hawaiian culture began in the late 1960s and continues to this day, with music playing a major role. The Brothers Cazimero, Hoʻokena, the late Israel Kamakawiwoʻole, and Mauiʻs own Kealiʻi Reichel have combined their voices with modern instruments and classic Hawaiian poetic techniques to create a magnificent new sound.

8 Slack-Key Guitar

The term slack-key refers to a style of playing guitar whereby the strings are loosened, producing a jangly sound. Gabby Pahinui was, perhaps, the most famous of Hawaii's slack-key masters – others included Raymond Kane and Sonny Chillingworth.

Musician playing the slack-key guitar

9 Steel Guitar

The Hawaiian steel guitar was born around the turn of the 20th century, but exactly where, when, and how is still a point of discussion. The instrument is held horizontally on the player's lap, and a sliding steel bar is used instead of fingers on the fret board. The sound was particularly big during the Sweet Leilani era.

10 World Beat

As a miscellany of musical styles from around the world has made its way to the islands, so it is increasingly influencing musicians. Jawaiian describes a blend of reggae and Hawaiian music, and island rappers are now putting their own slant on hip-hop music.

TOP 10 HAWAIIAN MUSIC AND DANCE ESSENTIALS

Traditional hula instruments

1 Pahu
Perhaps the most sacred of hula implements, *pahu* are drums that are traditionally made using coconut tree trunk with a covering of sharkskin.

2 Ipu
A hollowed-out gourd that, in skilled hands, is used to keep the beat in hula.

3 ʻIliʻili
Smooth stones – two are held in each hand and played by hula dancers in a style similar to Spanish castanets.

4 Pūʻili
Bamboo sticks, one end of each cut into a fringe so that they produce a rattling sound when played by hula dancers.

5 Kālaʻau
Sticks of varying length that are struck against each other during dancing.

6 ʻUliʻuli
Gourd shakers that are filled with seeds and usually topped with feathers.

7 Ukulele
A gift from the Portuguese that's now integral to modern Hawaiian music. "Jumping flea" was how Hawaiians first described the sound.

8 Guitar
Whether slack-key, steel, acoustic, or electric, the guitar is essential to Hawaiian music.

9 Standing Bass
As in jazz ensembles, the standing bass has found its way into much contemporary Hawaiian music.

10 Falsetto Voice
Most easily described as male vocalists singing above their regular range, there is arguably no sweeter sound than the Hawaiian falsetto.

Traditional Crafts

1 Weaving

Traditionally, women are the weavers in Hawaii. Many of the old everyday objects they created from *lau hala* (leaves of the pandanus tree) and the minutely thin *makaloa* (sedge grass) are considered works of art today. *Lau hala* mats, hats, and bags are easily found in craft shops, but *makaloa* is now something of a rarity.

Local woman weaving *lau hala* items

2 Lei Making

There's no more enduring symbol of Hawaii than the *lei* (garland). In the past, permanent *lei* were made from shells, seeds, bone, and feathers, and temporary *lei* from vines and leaves. Today, colorful and fragrant flowers such as plumeria and tuberose are most associated with this craft.

3 Heirloom Jewelry

A distinctive style of engraved jewelry, made popular by Queen Lili'oukalani, began in Hawaii in the 1800s. It was inspired by English Victorian gold jewelry adorned with black enamel and carved with floral, vine, and scroll designs. Island jewelers continue to make this style in many different forms.

4 Kapa

Used throughout old Polynesia for clothing, blankets, and decoration, Hawaiian *kapa* is made from the bark of the *wauke*, or paper mulberry tree. The process, which is restricted to women, involves pounding the bark repeatedly into paper-thin sheets that are then decorated using bamboo tools and plant dyes.

5 Hula Implements

The implements used by hula dancers and their accompanying chanters have changed little over hundreds of years. Though some enthusiasts still craft their own implements, hula supply shops on all the islands now allow dancers with busy 21st-century lives to purchase many of the items needed (though the materials used may not always be traditional these days).

6 Quilting

Among the many traditions introduced by the missionaries was quilting. Not surprisingly, Hawaiian women took to the art form and made it their own, replacing New England designs with gorgeous renderings of local flora and fauna.

Quilt with the Hawaiian flag and crest

Ukuleles for sale in a shop

7 Ukulele Making

A Portuguese import of the late 19th century, the ukulele quickly found its place in Hawaiian music. Ukulele making is a respected art in Hawaii, and companies like Kamaka on Oʻahu and Mele Ukulele on Maui handcraft high-quality instruments.

8 Featherwork

Cloaks, *lei*, and headware for the *aliʻi* (chief) were all once made with feathers. Birds were trapped so that specific feathers could be plucked before they were released. Yellow, red, and black were the colors most often used. Today, artisans still craft *lei* of feathers from pheasant and other species.

Royal cloak fashioned with bird feathers

9 Fishing Nets

Olonā fiber, derived from a native shrub, was commonly used in the old days to make fishing nets (a practice performed only by men). Man-made materials such as nylon replaced *olonā* in the 20th century.

10 Canoe Building

There is a great deal of ritual surrounding the building of a canoe, another of the men's arts. Canoes are traditionally made of *koa* and always from one log, carefully selected by the boat builder. The craft is still very much alive today.

TOP 10 LEI STYLES

1 Haku
Flowers, leaves, or fruit are braided onto three strands of *ti* or other natural fiber. *Haku lei* are most often worn around the head or on a hat.

2 Hili
Hili are braided *lei* made from a single plant material such as *ti* leaf or *maile*.

3 Humupapa
Flowers are sewn onto plant material such as dried banana leaves *(lau hala)*.

4 Kui
This is today's most familiar *lei* and consists of flowers strung together with needle and thread.

5 Kīpuʻu
Long-stemmed leaves or short lengths of vines are knotted together.

6 Wili
Plant materials are attached to a natural backing by winding fiber around them. *Wili lei* have no knots until the very end.

7 Lei Hulu (Feather Lei)
Traditionally made of feathers from now mostly extinct or endangered native birds, the art continues using feathers from common birds.

8 Lei Pūpū (Shell Lei)
These range from *puka-shell lei*, wildly popular in the 1970s, to museum-quality *Niʻihau-shell lei*, worth many thousands of dollars.

9 Seed Lei
Simple, single-stranded Job's Tears and intricately crafted *wiliwili-seed lei* are popular examples of this type.

10 Contemporary Lei
From silk and ribbon to yarn, currency, and even candy, contemporary *lei* are made for every occasion.

Brightly colored *lei*

TOP 10 Natural Wonders

The lighthouse at Diamond Head

1 Diamond Head Crater

Arguably Hawaii's most recognizable landmark, this volcanic remnant was named Leʻahi, "brow of the yellowfin tuna," for its shape. Its English name refers to the glinting calcite minerals, which were mistaken for diamonds. The interior has housed military operations and hosted rock concerts. A trail offers sweeping views (see p27).

2 Punchbowl

MAP L1 ■ Cemetery open 8am–6:30pm daily (Oct–Apr: to 5:30pm) ■ American Legion tours; adm; 532 3720

The 150,000-year-old cone above the city of Honolulu has three identities. Its Hawaiian name, Pūowaina, means "hill of sacrifice" – it was an ancient place of ritual and royal burial. Punchbowl, its English name, refers to its shape. Today it is also the final resting place of more than 35,000 veterans of American wars in Asia and the Pacific.

3 Waiʻanae Mountain Range

MAP B3–4

Composed of the remnants of the Waiʻanae volcano, said to have become dormant 2.5 million years ago, this range is the higher of the two on Oʻahu, reaching above 4,000 ft (1,219 m). The mountains here have a distinct wet (east) and dry (west) side.

4 Manoa Falls Trail

MAP E5 ■ End of Mānoa Rd, Mānoa Valley ■ 587 4175 ■ Open dawn–dusk ■ www.hawaiitrails.org

A gently sloping but rocky and muddy trail winds through groves of bamboo, eucalyptus, edible mountain apple, and tangled hau trees. The 150-ft (46-m) waterfall at the end is spectacular after a heavy rainfall. There's no fee for the hike, but parking is $5.

5 Hanauma Bay

MAP F6 ■ 396 4229 ■ Open 6am–7pm Wed–Mon ■ Adm ■ Access denied when lot is full; go early or after 2pm

This keyhole-shaped Nature Preserve is so beautiful and popular that the state has had to restrict

Pristine Hanauma Bay

access to protect it.
Visitors enter through an
informative Marine
Education Center and
must view a video before
descending to the bay via
shuttle bus for snorkeling
and sunbathing.

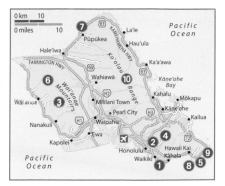

6 Mount Ka'ala
MAP B3

This, the tallest peak
on O'ahu at 4,020 ft
(1,225 m), is a preserve
where indigenous birds
and boggy plants prosper
in the mist. On its slopes and at its
feet, sandalwood once prospered,
before the forests were decimated by
Hawaiian royalty to pay for Chinese
silks and other trade goods.

Bodyboarder at the Banzai Pipeline

7 Banzai Pipeline

Just off 'Ehukai Beach Park,
the Banzai Pipeline is the name
given to a spectacular winter surf
break, the result of a shallow
coral reef that serves as a sudden
stopping point for deep water
currents sweeping inland. The name
Banzai comes from the battle cry of
Japanese warriors, and was first
applied to the waves here during
the narration of the late 1950s film
Surf Safari (see p82).

8 Koko Head
MAP F6

Although not the most impressive
peak on O'ahu, Koko' Head's homely
bulk is a landmark. Nearby, Koko
Crater rises to 1,000 ft (366 m). A
panoramic 2-mile (3-km) hike is

reached through a botanical park –
the windswept, narrow, and crumbly
trail is challenging.

9 Hālona Blow Hole
MAP F5

A lava tube that funnels geysers
of sea water high into the air, this
dramatic feature is one to observe
with care, preferably from the scenic
pullout above it. Many who have
ventured too near have been injured
or killed. From November through
March, watch for spouting whales
out to sea, as well as spouting water.

10 Ko'olau Mountain Range
MAP C2–D4

The wind- and water-cut Ko'olaus
are the subject of countless Hawaiian
chants and songs. This Windward-
side mountain range (the name
means "windward"), so green and
dramatic, forms O'ahu's spine from
southeast to northwest.

Luxuriant Ko'olau Mountain Range

🔟 Gardens and Nature Parks

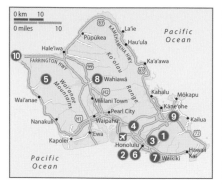

Hawaii. It includes some of the oldest trees on the island, a superb collection of orchids, and rare and endangered tropical plants (see pp22–3).

③ Hawai'i Nature Center
MAP C6 ▪ 2131 Makiki Heights Dr, Honolulu ▪ 955 0100

This non-profit conservation group encourages children to look after the environment. Weekend family programs – including interpretive hikes, earth care projects, and nature adventures – are held at the center, located in a picturesque ravine in Makiki Valley.

① Lyon Arboretum
MAP C6 ▪ 3860 Mānoa Rd, Honolulu ▪ 988 0456 ▪ Open 8am–4pm Mon–Fri, 9am–3pm Sat ▪ www.manoa.hawaii.edu/lyonarboretum

Named for Harold L. Lyon, longtime director of botanical gardens in Honolulu, this university facility is both a field station and a public garden of tropical plants, native plants, conservation biology, and Hawaiian ethnobotany. Classes, workshops, and outings are offered.

② Foster Botanical Gardens

Planted by a pioneering botanist in the 1850s, nurtured by an amateur gardener from the 1880s, and donated to the city in 1931, this is the oldest botanical garden in

④ Moanalua Gardens
MAP D5 ▪ 1352 Pineapple Place, Honolulu ▪ 839 5334

This non-profit environmental education center in historic Kamananui Valley offers walks and operates an award-winning school program. The free Prince Lot Hula Festival (see p64) takes place each July on a traditional grassy hula pā (mound) in the shady park.

⑤ Mount Ka'ala Natural Area Reserve
MAP B3

This reserve sits alongside a military reservation and is easily reached by road. However, the paved route is off-limits to civilians, who must climb challenging trails to reach the misty bog in a bowl-like hollow atop O'ahu's highest peak. The area has become a safe haven for native plants and wildlife; a boardwalk allows viewing without causing damage to the fragile ecosystems. It's best to consult detailed hiking guides before setting out.

Gazebo in Foster Botanical Gardens

Stream and waterfall in Lili'uokalani Botanical Gardens

6 Lili'uokalani Botanical Gardens

Bequeathed to her people in 1958 by the last reigning monarch of Hawaii, this is a tranquil retreat in the busy city, and is devoted entirely to native Hawaiian plants. The site encompasses portions of Nu'uanu Valley, including Nu'uanu Stream and Waikahalulu Waterfall (see p72).

7 Honolulu Zoo

The venerable zoological garden in Waikīkī incorporates savanna and tropical forest areas, birds and reptiles of the Pacific islands, and a children's zoo. A summer concert series is hosted here (see pp26–7).

Flamingo at Honolulu Zoo

8 Wahiawā Botanical Gardens

Opened in 1957, this rainforest garden nestles in 27 acres (11 ha) between two mountain ranges. Used as an arboretum by sugar planters in the 1920s, it is considered the "tropical jewel" of the Honolulu Botanical Gardens (see p93).

9 Kawainui Marsh
MAP E4

Rescued from development proposals in the 1960s, this 830-acre (336-ha) wetland offers abundant wildlife, including waterbirds, fish,

and other aquatic life, as well as archaeological sites. Access is available from a flood control dike but the city is contemplating an ambitious perimeter.

10 Ka'ena Point Natural Area Reserve
MAP A2

Largely unimproved and subject to the pressures of multiple uses such as off-road vehicles, fishermen, hikers, shell-collectors, and traditional Hawaiian practitioners, Ka'ena Point park is a narrow strip of land that connects the two ends of Farrington Highway (at Mokule'ia and Yokohama Bay). Hike a muddy, rutted road, catching sight of small bays and beaches until you reach O'ahu's end, a tumbled landscape of sand dunes, rocks, and waves.

Ka'ena Point Natural Area Reserve

🔟 Treks

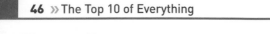

Expansive vistas from the Diamond Head State Monument viewpoint

1 Diamond Head Trail
MAP C7 ■ The trail begins at the Diamond Head State Monument parking lot, off Diamond Head Rd at 18th St in Kaimukī

Very steep in places, dusty and dark in others, this 0.8-mile (1.2-km) hike ends in a series of viewing platforms. The landscape before you, from Koko Head in the east to the curve of the Leeward Coast on the west, is worth the energy expended.

Trail leading to Makapu'u Lighthouse

2 Makapu'u Lighthouse Trail
MAP F5 ■ Park at the Makapu'u Wayside

Makapu'u Point is the spot where prevailing currents from the deep ocean are split by the land, resulting in interesting wave action. An easy but breezy 1-mile (1.6-km) walk along an abandoned road leads to a World War II pillbox and Makapu'u Lighthouse. Watch for whales in winter.

3 Judd Memorial Trail
MAP E5 ■ Reached from Nu'uanu Pali Drive near Ilanawai Condominium

This easy one-hour trek in Nu'uanu Valley is a tribute to the forester Charles S. Judd, who planted the pines here in the 1930s. The pond is less picturesquely named Jackass Ginger after a donkey that used to be tethered in a nearby ginger grove.

4 Makiki Valley Loop Trail
MAP C6 ■ Enter via Hawaii Nature Center, off Makiki Heights Dr

This 2-mile (3-km) loop, incorporating short segments of three longer routes – Kane'aole Trail, Makiki Valley Trail, and Maunalaha Trail – has been cleared, planted with native vegetation, and equipped with directional signs.

5 Honolulu Walking Tours
AIA: 545 4242 ■ Hawaii Heritage Center: 521 2749 ■ Ohana Tours: 866 204 7331

The American Institute of Architects (AIA) leads two-hour Saturday tours (starting at 9am) of downtown Honolulu, taking in examples of various architectural styles. Chinatown tours are led by the Hawaii Heritage Center on Wednesdays and Fridays (9:30–11:30am). Ohana Tours also offers walking tours of Chinatown and downtown Honolulu on weekday mornings.

6 Lulumahu Falls Trail

MAP E5 ■ End of Old Pali Rd, off Pali Hwy ■ Open dawn to dusk

This trail that leads to a beautiful waterfall is fairly short (less than a mile) but challenging, and best suited to skilled hikers. The streamside trail is slippery and muddy and takes you through dense bamboo forest, past the Nu'uanu Reservoir, and close to the ghostly, crumbling Kaniakapupu Ruins.

7 Maunawili Demonstration Trail

MAP F4

Requiring half a day and someone to pick you up at the end, the Maunawili Trail extends from Pali Highway above Kailua to a back road in Waimānalo. It is a moderately easy 10-mile (16-km) hike for which

you will be rewarded with a rainforest valley, then views of the island's windward side.

8 Kualoa Ranch Horse Trails

MAP E3 ■ 49-560 Kamehameha Hwy, Kāne'ohe ■ 237 7321 ■ www.kualoa. com

The Kualoa Ranch & Activity Club offers daily one- and two-hour rides on this historic, 150-year-old family ranch (see p98). One-hour rides traverse the base of the Ko'olau Mountains; two-hour rides delve into wide Ka'a'awa Valley. These are suitable for inexperienced riders.

9 Ka'ena Point Trail

MAP A2 ■ The trailhead is at the Mokulē'ia end of Farrington Hwy

This 5-mile (8-km), two-hour trek along the muddy remains of the shore highway offers pole-fishing sites, shelling in small inlets during low tide, and glimpses of birds, dolphins, and whales (see p84).

10 'Aiea Loop Trail

MAP D4 ■ From the top of 'Aiea Heights Dr, enter Keaīwa State Park and park at the top

A family-friendly hike in and out of the gullies in 'Aiea Valley will familiarize you with vegetation such as 'uluhe fern and 'ōhi'a lehua. (Don't pick the scarlet sprays of lehua flowers, custom says, or it will rain.)

On Maunawili Demonstration Trail

🔟 Beaches

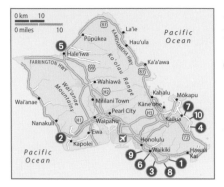

extremely limited, so arrive early or consider taking public transit.

3 Sans Souci
MAP E6

Sprung around a small resort where Robert Louis Stevenson stayed in the 1880s, Sans Souci white sand beach is good for swimming, body-surfing, and boogie boarding. Safe, calm, and shallow, it's popular with families.

1 Waiʻalae Beach County Park
MAP E6

More popular for weddings and picnics than it is for swimming, this Kāhala beach is hemmed in by coral but offers access to coveted wind-surfing areas and fishing holes. Watch out for – and keep small children away from – the deep, sometimes fast-flowing channel cut by Waiʻalae Stream as it enters the sea.

2 Ko Olina Beach Park
MAP B5 ■ Kapolei

Four postcard-perfect lagoons fringed by powdery soft sand provide shallow, calm blue waters for swim-ming and snorkeling. For visitors who are not staying at any of the nearby luxury resorts, parking is

4 Bellows Field Beach County Park

Open to the public on weekends and national holidays, this beach park within a military reservation is prized for its broad shelf of powder-fine white sand, turquoise waters, and ironwood-shaded campgrounds (camping is by permit only). It is ideal for swimmers and novice surfers, but watch out for jellyfish (see p104).

5 Haleʻiwa Aliʻi
MAP B2

This beach park is popular for family picnics, swimming, and surfing offshore at Puaʻena Point. The site has restrooms, a shady pavilion, plenty of food concessions, life-guards, and sports fields, too.

Palm-backed bay in Ko Olina Beach Park

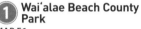

Waikīkī beach, lined with hotels

6 Waikīkī Beach

Possibly the most famous beach in the world, Waikīkī has a lovely beach promenade, an eye-catching waterfall feature, and lush, grassy berms to block street noise. The beach remains prime people-watching territory, as well as being a gentle and safe place for swimming, snorkeling, and learning to surf *(see p78)*.

7 Kailua Beach Park
MAP F4

Around 2 miles (3 km) of golden sand fringe Kailua Bay, which is divided into three sections. The northernmost beaches, Oneawa (with roadside parking) and Kalama (which has a parking lot), are accessed through Kailua neighborhoods. Kailua Beach Park has parking lots, food concessions, a volleyball court, picnic tables, and lifeguard towers. You can surf, windsurf, swim, boat, kayak, canoe, snorkel, and dive here, and the view of Nā Mokulua ("the mokes," as locals call these tiny islets) is the icing on the cake.

8 Ka'alāwai Beach
MAP E6

Reached from a public right of way at the end of Kulamanu Place off Kāhala Avenue and Diamond Head Road, this narrow, white-sand beach is protected by a reef and is safe for swimming and snorkeling. It's also used for diving, pole fishing, and throw-netting, while surfers make spectacular use of breaks in the reef.

9 Ala Moana
MAP B6

The most popular beach park in urban Honolulu offers 76 acres (31 ha) of activities, though most people simply swim, wade, and sunbathe on the man-made sandy beach. If you do swim here, you must take care, as the channel is deep and, at low tide, you don't have to venture far to be caught in strong currents. Facilities onshore include food concessions, tennis courts, lifeguard towers, and softball fields.

White-sand Lanikai Beach on O'ahu

10 Lanikai Beach
MAP F4

Frequently voted one of the world's best beaches, Lanikai can be reached through beach access trails in the ritzy Lanikai neighborhood along Mokulua Drive. The beach is flat and sandy, quite narrow in spots, and popular for such activities as swimming, boating, diving, and snorkeling.

🔟 Surfing Beaches

Riding a wave at Point Panic

for swimming, kayaking, and snorkeling. Come October through to April, it is crowded with open-mouthed visitors watching surfers from around the world ride the wild surf *(see p84)*.

① Kaka'ako Waterfront Park/Point Panic
MAP B6

Unless you're highly skilled on a board and ready to join the elite who paddle out to Point Panic every day, this park is strictly for spectators. There's no beach, swimming is dangerous because the break crashes into the retaining wall, and sharks haunt the area. However, a broad pathway extends the length of the park offering great views, and picnic pavilions are clustered along it. This is also a favorite spot for watching celebratory firework displays over Waikīkī.

② Ala Moana Beach
MAP B6

This area is popular for surfing because it offers a range of challenges from easy and slow Canoes to the more frisky Queen's, Paradise, and Populars areas. Locals who work in Waikīkī hit the waves before and after work.

③ Waimea Bay

Captain Cook first landed on O'ahu at Waimea Bay. A beach with two personalities, it is calm as a bathtub in summer, making it ideal

④ Sunset Beach
MAP C1

In winter, this wide golden strand is piled high, forming a steep, natural amphitheater for watching surfers attack the awesome waves. In summer, changing tides flatten the beach out, making it more sunbather-friendly. All year long, though, dangerous currents make swimming risky. There are park facilities across the street.

Stretch of golden sand at Sunset Beach

⑤ Makapu'u Beach Park
MAP F5

The slow rolling shoulders of the waves and the lack of a reef below make this spot ideal for bodysurfing. Board surfing is prohibited to prevent collisions. Watch out during high winter surf, and heed flag warnings from the lifeguards *(see p103)*.

6 ʻEhukai Beach Park
MAP C1

ʻEhukai ("sea spray" in Hawaiian) is safe for swimming during spring and summer, but in fall and winter the board surfers take over and it becomes the viewing stand for observing the action at the famous Banzai Pipeline to the left of the beach park.

7 Banzai Pipeline
A shallow coral reef extending out from the beach fronting Ke Nui Road throws up waves of tremendous power and steepness – so powerful that no one thought they could be ridden until the 1960s. Injuries from wiping out on the reef are numerous, but surfers can't resist these monsters. "Banzai" was the final battle cry of Japanese kamikaze pilots *(see p82)*.

8 Sandy Beach
"Sandy's" is the bodyboarding capital of Oʻahu and is popular with surfers. Unfortunately, it is also the site of many serious accidents and frequent rescues. A steep drop-off at the sand's edge means that waves are always pounding here, so only the most experienced should take on this surf, and everyone should take care of the treacherous backwash, which frequently catches waders off-guard *(see pp104–5)*.

Surfers enjoying the waves at Sandy Beach

9 Kaʻena Point State Park
MAP A2 ■ Reached via a 2.5-mile (4-km) walk

Until the introduction of tow-in surfing, the mammoth waves of Kaʻena Point remained tantalizingly off limits to surfers because of the impossibility of paddling out from the rock-fringed, current-tossed shore. A north swell at Lae o Kaʻena results in 30–40-ft (9–12-m) waves and brings out the most daring surfers.

10 Mākaha Beach
Site of the Mākaha International Surfing Championships, the beach here is steep-sloped and wide, with plenty of golden sand and deep waters close to shore. The well-formed waves range from medium in the off-season to very large in the winter. Stray boards can be a hazard to swimmers *(see p93)*.

Outdoor Activities

① Gliding and Skydiving at Mokulēʻia

Dillingham Airfield past Waialua on Farrington Hwy, Rte 930, at Mokulēʻia
Air adventures at Dillingham Airfield include gliding, skydiving, and scenic flights *(see p85)*. Choose from a 20-minute single-person glider flight to long scenic flights and lessons.

② CLIMB Works – Keana Farms

MAP D1 ▪ 1 Enos Rd, Kahuku ▪ 200 7906 ▪ www.climbworks.com
Learn about Hawaii's history and culture while taking in amazing ocean and mountain views during an exhilarating three-hour zipline tour of a working agricultural farm on Oʻahu's North Shore.

③ Jet Skiing at Maunalua Bay

Jet-powered personal watercraft are similar to motocycles and offer a noisy but enjoyable way to skim over the water. By law, jet skis are restricted to weekday, daytime hours. Ask about ski/parasailing combo packages.

④ Guided Hikes

 Three non-profit groups – the Sierra Club (538 6616), The Nature Conservancy (537 4508), and Hawaiian Trail and Mountain Club (674 1459) – offer hikes, with the last group definitely on the hardier side.

Parasailing over the sea at Waikīkī

⑤ Parasailing at Waikīkī

Hundreds of visitors a day experience the thrill of parasailing – sitting, strapped in a harness attached to a parachute, pulled by a boat, high above the waves.

⑥ Kayaking Kailua and Kāneʻohe

Locals favor kayaking along the Windward Coast, where small islets offer interesting scenery, and there's a popular sandbar in Kāneʻohe Bay. However, many of the islets are bird sanctuaries where landing is prohibited.

Kayaking along the Windward Coast near Kailua

⑦ Walking Tours

Regular walking tours of downtown, Chinatown, the Capitol District, Waikīkī, and the University campus are offered by various non-profit groups (see pp46–7). A free map, the *Waikīkī Historic Trail*, offers a self-guided tour.

⑧ The Lūʻau Experience

Paradise Cove Lūʻau: Ko Olina; 842 5911 ▪ Germaine's Lūʻau: 91–119 Olai St, Kapolei; 949 6626 ▪ Royal Lūʻau at the Royal Hawaiian Hotel: Waikīkī; 931 7194; Mon only

To experience an authentic Hawaiian feast (*lūʻau*), it's best to find a local family giving one. If that's not possible, try the Polynesian Cultural Center (see pp32–3) or other commercial operations.

Playing polo at Waimānalo

⑨ Polo at Waimānalo and Mokulēʻia

Honolulu Polo Club: Waimānalo Polo Grounds (across from Bellows Beach) ▪ Mokulēʻia Polo Club: 411 Farrington Hwy in Mokulēʻia

Polo came to Hawaii with the moneyed elite, and two polo grounds operate on Oʻahu. Matches are held at 2pm on Sundays (Jun–Oct).

⑩ Bike Hawaii

MAP D5 ▪ Honolulu area ▪ 734 4214 ▪ www.bikehawaii.com

Fun, knowledgeable guides lead mountain biking tours through rainforests and valleys, passing waterfalls, villages, and World War II relics. Biking tours can be combined with snorkeling, hiking, and kayaking.

TOP 10 RENTAL PLACES AND COMMERCIAL TOURS

Kids on stand-up paddle boards

1 Rainbow Watersports
372 9304 ▪ www.rainbow watersports.com
A stand-up paddle surf school.

2 Island Seaplane
836 6273 ▪ www.islandseaplane.com
This company has experienced pilots and certified instructors.

3 Skydive Hawaii
637 9700 ▪ www.skydivehawaii.com
Flights for experienced and novice skydivers at Dillingham Airfield.

4 Hawaiian Parasail
591 1280 ▪ www.hawaiianpara sail.com
Daily flights depart from Kewalo Basin. Free pickup from Waikīkī hotels.

5 X-Treme Parasail
737 3599 ▪ www.xtremeparasail.com
This company offers parasailing, fishing expeditions, jet ski rentals, and more.

6 H2O Sports
396 0100 ▪ www.h2osportshawaii. com
Operator based at Maunalua Bay.

7 Hawaii Water Sports Center
395 3773 ▪ www.hawaiiwatersports center.com
Offering a variety of rental equipment.

8 Twogood Kayaks Hawaii
262 5656 ▪ www.twogoodkayaks.com
Reputable firm on the Windward Coast.

9 Kailua Sailboards and Kayaks
262 2555 ▪ www.kailuasail boards.com
Ideal for sailboard and kayak hire.

10 Hawaii Ecotourism Association
235 5431 ▪ www.hawaiiecotourism. org
For commercial operations offering guided hikes, consult this association.

🔟 Golf Courses

The challenging terrain around the 18th hole at Ko Olina Golf Course

① Ko Olina Golf Course
MAP B5 ■ 92–1220 Ali'inui Dr, Kapolei ■ 676 5300 Ext. 1

This emerald oasis carved out of a dusty plain by designer Ted Robinson is considered one of O'ahu's most challenging and beautiful courses, featuring water features and black swans. Although expensive, it offers plenty of discounts.

② Royal Hawaiian Golf Club
MAP F4 ■ 770 Auloa Rd, Kailua ■ 262 2139

Hidden at the base of the Ko'olau Mountains, in the paradise-like Maunawili Valley, this scenic Greg Norman-designed 18-hole golf course features swaying palms, fish-filled ponds and streams, and plenty of challenges. Expect to lose more than a few balls in the ravines and surrounding rainforest.

③ 'Ewa Beach Golf Club
MAP C5 ■ 91–050 Ft. Weaver Rd, 'Ewa Beach ■ 689 6565

This enjoyable semiprivate course designed by Robin Nelson manages to retain the character of the historic dryland 'Ewa Plain with its *kiawe* trees and preserved archaeological sites. The tight, manicured fairways and ubiquitous bunkers offer a fair challenge-to-reward ratio.

④ Hawaii Prince Golf Course
MAP C5 ■ 91–1200 Ft. Weaver Rd, 'Ewa Beach ■ 944 4567

Affiliated with the Hawaii Prince Hotel, and played frequently by visitors from Japan, this Arnold Palmer-designed course offers 27 subtly challenging holes. The flattish terrain is bedeviled by winds, tight fairways, and lots of water.

⑤ Ko'olau Golf Club
MAP E4 ■ 45–550 Kiona'ole Rd, Kāne'ohe, 247 7088

Golfers travel a long and winding road at this course, nestled among

Lush hills of Ko'olau Golf Club

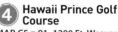

the foothills of the dramatic Koʻolau mountain range. It has been rated among the top 100 courses by *Golf Magazine* and named Oʻahu's best by *Golf Digest*. Be sure to bring plenty of extra golf balls and prepare for long holes, water hazards, and a difficult layout.

6 Pali Golf Course

MAP E4 ■ 45-050 Kamehameha Hwy ■ 266 7612

In the absence of water hazards and bunkers, the challenge of this undulating landscape is wet and often windy weather. But even duffers can enjoy meandering down swale and up hillside on sunny days.

7 The Golf Courses at Turtle Bay

MAP C1 ■ 57-091 Kamehameha Hwy, Kahuku ■ 293 8574

Two courses are showcased on this 880-acre (356 ha) resort on Oʻahu's remote North Shore. The George Fazio Course has wide fairways and deep bunkers; the Arnold Palmer Course incorporates a "tropical links" of sun, wind, and sand on the front nine and a forested upland nine on the back.

8 Hawaii Kai Championship Golf Course

MAP F5 ■ 8902 Kalanianaʻole Hwy, Maunalua ■ 395 2358

This coastal course is a windswept beauty, with narrow fairways, plenty of sand, and an ocean view from every tee. Be sure to sign your name on the leaves of the *milo* or "message" tree. A shorter Executive Course is also available.

9 Olomana Golf Links

MAP F5 ■ 41-1801 Kalanianaʻole Hwy, Waimānalo ■ 259 7926

Though it's called a links, this much-played windward side course is

in view of, but not right by, the ocean. It's a pretty place to play golf, with the mountains as a backdrop and a network of ponds, but keep your eye on the ball and watch out for the little lakes.

Putting at Ala Wai Golf Course

10 Ala Wai Golf Course

MAP L5 ■ 404 Kapahulu Ave, Waikīkī ■ 737 7387

The world's busiest course is also one of the most loved in Hawaii for its balance of challenge and playability – tradewinds may beat your ball back and slow play can test your patience, but the course is flat, there's not much water, and it is frequented by many friendly locals.

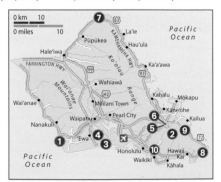

🔟 Spas and Fitness Centers

A massage cabana at elegant SpaHalekulani

opportunity to work up a sweat. There are three clubs in Honolulu, one in Waikīkī, and four others dotted around Oʻahu; most offer short-term passes.

④ Laʻakea Spa Hawaiʻi
2169 Kālia Rd, Diamond Head Tower ▪ 926 2882 ▪ www.laakeaspahawaii. com
Located in the Outrigger Reef on the Beach hotel (see p116), the Laʻakea Spa offers guests relaxing poolside massages. It also offers a range of pampering packages designed to make guests feel like aliʻi (royalty). You can charge the spa services to your room if you're a guest at any of the 20 Outrigger or ʻOhana properties in Hawaii.

① SpaHalekulani
2199 Kālia Rd ▪ 931 5322 ▪ www.halekulani.com
Luxury hotel Halekulani's in-house spa SpaHalekulani uses authentic Polynesian therapeutic rituals with top-notch products and proven techniques. It offers an extensive range of massages, treatments, and hair and nail care services.

② Paul Brown Salon and Day Spa
800 338 0033 ▪ www.paulbrown salons.com
Two of Paul Brown's locations, one at the Victoria Ward Center in Honolulu and the other at Kailua, are arguably the best of the independent day spas on Oʻahu.

③ 24-Hour Fitness
923 9090 ▪ www.24Hour Fitness.com
As the name implies, this national chain offers a round-the-clock

⑤ Heaven on Earth Salon and Day Spa
Bishop Square, 1050 Alakea St ▪ 599 5501 ▪ www.heavenonearth hawaii.com
The place of respite for harried downtown workers is equally agreeable to harried tourists in need of a stress-relieving massage. Owner Lora Nakai wants the feeling of wellness to last, and she encourages therapists to impart helpful tips to clients.

⑥ Clark Hatch Physical Fitness Center
745 Fort St ▪ 536 7205 ▪ www. clarkhatch.com.my
With a network of centers throughout Asia and the Pacific, founder Clark Hatch's philosophy is "total fitness." Trained instructors create individual programs to promote a lifetime of well-being.

(7) Laka Skin Care and Spa
320 Ward Ave, Suite 200
■ 397 5252 ■ www.lakaspa.com

Diminutive, but widely recognized as among the best in Honolulu, Laka's self-declared aim is to improve the clients' spiritual and physical health through a range of organic, nourishing and environmentally friendly skin and body treatments.

(8) Aloha Healing Arts
1831 Ala Moana Blvd, No. 202
■ 386 1820 ■ www.alohahealingarts.com

A skilled massage therapist with almost two decades of experience, Fran Rose offers Swedish massage, reflexology, shiatsu, sports massage, acupressure, and iridology.

(9) Marsha Nadalin Salon & Spa
Kahala Mall ■ 737 8505

If chic and upscale Kahala Mall is on your list of shopping stops, you can be rejuvenated at this day spa located in the shopping center. Men's services are available, too.

(10) Sunset Yoga Hawaii
2699 Kalākaua Ave ■ 321 3297
■ www.sunsetyogahawaii.com

An expert yoga instructor provides group and individual classes on Waikīkī Beach and beyond. All levels are welcome.

Class with Sunset Yoga Hawaii

TOP 10 HEALTH AND BEAUTY TREATMENTS

Pōhaku (stones), used for massages

1 Massage
Shiatsu, Swedish, and Thai styles are available, but why not try Hawaii's traditional *lomilomi* or the newer *Pōhaku* (stone) massage.

2 Steam/Sauna
The steam room is wet, the sauna dry, and either one will open the body's pores in readiness for other treatments.

3 Botanical Baths
Aromatherapy oils, herbs, and seaweeds are added to whirlpool tubs to either calm or re-energize the body.

4 Herbal Scrubs
Scrubs use ingredients such as native red clay and island sea salts to exfoliate, detoxify, and soften the skin.

5 Herbal Wraps
Wraps use a great variety of herbs and the application of heat to draw out impurities from the skin.

6 Facials
Designed to clean and rehydrate the face; choices depend on skin type and individual needs.

7 Aromatherapy
Integrated into many spa treatments, natural fragrances are used to invoke a specific mood or feeling.

8 Manicure/Pedicure
The perfect way to end a day at the spa, manicures and pedicures always include a quick hand and/or foot massage.

9 Makeup
Every salon has experts on hand for a professional application of makeup.

10 Fitness
All gyms and many spas have work-out machines, free weights, pools, and fitness classes.

Local Dishes

1 Kālua Pork

The centerpiece of any *lū'au*, or feast, is a whole pig, slow-roasted (*kālua*) in an underground oven. The meat literally falls from the bones. This cooking method also works with turkey, squash, and sweet potatoes.

Hawaiian *poke* bowl with raw tuna

2 Sushi, Sashimi, and Poke

The primary Japanese culinary influences are sashimi (sliced raw fish) and sushi (raw fish, shellfish, or vegetables, served on top of, or rolled with, rice). *Poke*, the Hawaiian word for diced or chopped, is Hawaii's version of Latin American *ceviche*. These delicious raw fish-based dishes are available everywhere – from fine dining restaurants to local supermarkets.

3 Poi

The staple of the Hawaiian diet, *poi* is made by pounding the corm of the *taro* or *kalo* plant to a paste, a

task that is strictly a male preserve. Traditional Hawaiians believe their culture to be descended from a *kalo* plant, signifying the symbolic importance of this food.

4 Kimchi

Introduced by Hawaii's Korean immigrants, *kimchi* is simply pickled cabbage, but for those diners who love hot – that is, very hot – flavors, it is a "must try." Traditionally, the cabbage is stored in tightly sealed jars and buried in the ground, then dug up as and when needed.

5 Portuguese Sweet Bread and Bean Soup

Fresh from the oven and slathered with creamy butter is the best way to enjoy this wonderful bread, introduced by Hawaii's Portuguese immigrants. Originally baked in outdoor brick ovens, it is now available at markets throughout the islands. Every family in Hawaii has its own Portuguese bean soup recipe. Brimming with beans, meat, and vegetables, it can be a hearty meal in itself, especially when accompanied by a thick slice of sweet bread.

6 Plate Lunch

Meat, two scoops of rice, and macaroni salad are the three essential elements of the plate lunch. Sold on every street corner in Hawaii, it represents the melding of cultures. The meat comes in many varieties, from teriyaki beef to pork and chicken prepared in various ways.

A classic Hawaiian plate lunch

Saimin, a noodle dish similar to ramen

7 Noodles and Rice

Few meals in Hawaii are served without either rice or noodles. Noodles in hot broth with pork and green onions is a common dish for breakfast, lunch, or dinner, and left-over dinner rice often reappears as fried rice for the next day's breakfast.

8 Tropical Fruit

Mango, papaya, guava, *liliko'i* (passion fruit), bananas, and, of course, pineapple. Pure and simple fresh from the tree, blended into a delicious fruit smoothie, or transformed into an amazing dessert, these are truly heavenly flavors.

Pineapple smoothie

9 Shave Ice

It has other names in other places – snow cone is one – but it is simply small chips of ice, flavored with one or more of myriad syrups, served in a paper cone. Cool and refreshing on a hot summer day, the rainbow variety shave ice has become a virtual symbol of Hawaii.

10 Spam

One of the most maligned foods in history is one of Hawaii's most beloved. Canned Spiced Ham (SPAM) was a military staple because it can be kept for long periods of time. It is, perhaps, the large military presence in Hawaii that first accounted for its curious popularity in the islands.

TOP 10 LOCAL FOOD STOPS

1 Little Village Noodle House
MAP H3 = 1113 Smith St, Honolulu
The menu here offers a full range of regional Chinese specialties.

2 Gulick Delicatessen & Coffee Shop
MAP D5 = 1512 Gulick Ave, Honolulu
The quintessential plate-lunch eatery.

3 Side Street Inn
MAP E6 = 1225 Hopaka, Honolulu
After-work hangout of Honolulu's chefs, offering savory bar food.

4 Kaka'ako Kitchen
MAP G6 = 1200 Ala Moana Blvd, Honolulu
A plate-lunch venue owned by a high-end chef. It has great pastries, too.

5 Helena's Hawaiian Food
MAP D5 = 1240 N. School St, Honolulu
Helena's has made some of the best traditional Hawaiian food since 1946.

6 Tokkuri-Tei
MAP M7 = 449 Kapahulu Ave, Honolulu
A Japanese *izakaya* (tavern) with an innovative East-West menu.

7 Libby Manapua Shop
MAP B6 = 410 Kalihi St, Honolulu
Some of the best *manapua* (steamed pork buns) in O'ahu. Cash only.

8 Palace Saimin
MAP G1 = 1256 N. King St, Honolulu
Serving Hawaii's favorite comfort food: steaming bowls of noodles.

9 Zippy's Restaurants
This chain of O'ahu-style diners serves simple, hearty food *(see p107)*.

10 Rainbow Drive-In
MAP E6 = 3308 Kanaina Ave, Honolulu
This has long been a popular spot for plate lunches and Hawaiian staples.

Neon sign at the Rainbow Drive-In

⑩ Restaurants

The modern, light-filled interior of Koko Head Café

① Lucky Belly
The Asian fusion menu at this modern ramen joint is full of decadent and mouthwatering options. Japanese whisky and sake connoisseurs will not be disappointed by the selection available, either. Feeling hungry at 2am? Try Lucky Belly's late-night window for satisfying and surprisingly refined *pūpū* (appetizers) *(see p75)*.

② Sansei Seafood Restaurant & Sushi Bar
Sushi bar, fine dining restaurant, fashionable cocktail lounge, karaoke palace – Sansei is all of these. The name means "third generation" and implies the East-West sophistication that the grandchildren of the immigrant generation have achieved *(see p81)*.

Large sushi rolls at Sansei

③ Koko Head Café
Chef Lee Anne Wong creates rich breakfast dishes with Hawaiian and Asian flare – omelettes with miso-smoked pork and onion, bibimbap (mixed rice) with sausage and ham, and volcano eggs topped with spicy tomato sauce, cheese, and vegetables *(see p107)*.

④ Town
This island-inspired Italian bistro has a true farm-to-table menu. Fresh greens are paired with papaya, avocado, and pecans. Hand-cut pasta is topped with goat ragout and Parmesan cheese, while pork belly is served with polenta, bitter greens, macadamia nuts, and salsa verde. The desserts are not to be missed either *(see p75)*.

⑤ Alan Wong's Restaurant
Hailed by many people as Hawaii's best restaurant, Alan Wong's marries the spirit of local cultures with a formal setting. The colorful dishes – innovative seafood preparations and amazing sauces – are delicious; the atmosphere relaxed and convivial. It also has a great wine list *(see p75)*.

⑥ Mahina & Sun's
Elegant island cuisine made with organic, local, and sustainably sourced ingredients features on the

menu here. The vintage-inspired decor, from the wallpaper to the furniture, is also locally sourced. Try the Family Feast inside, or sip cool cocktails poolside *(see p81)*.

7 La Mer

Hawaii's best and most authentically French restaurant makes lavish use of both local seafood and imported delicacies to create "cuisine de soleil," a cuisine of the sun with a distinctly Provençal bent. Formal dress is required *(see p81)*.

8 The Pig and the Lady

A former pop-up and farmers' market stall, this family-run Vietnamese eatery in Chinatown serves delicious comfort food with a modern twist. Try the LFC (chicken wings), the Pho French Dip, and, for dessert, the house-special decadent Sundae Funday *(see p75)*.

The outdoor area at Roy's Restaurant

9 Roy's Restaurant

Roy Yamaguchi founded the first O'ahu restaurant of note in 1988. Here he offers the same spicy mixture that is his signature – creative cuisine influenced from around the Pacific Rim *(see p107)*.

10 DK Steak House

The Waikīkī Marriott hosts a steakhouse experience that rivals any in the state, complete with in-house dry aged beef and a unique wine list. When you reserve ask for a balcony table to enjoy breathtaking views of Waikīkī Beach while you dine *(see p81)*.

TOP 10 REGIONAL INGREDIENTS

Papayas and lychees at a market

1 Tropical Fruit
Chefs make excellent use of pineapple, papaya, guava, *liliko'i*, and lychee in salsas, sauces, and desserts.

2 Local Greens
Small farms grow dozens of varieties of lettuce and greens for use in the restaurants of Hawaii.

3 Vine-Ripened Tomatoes
Much juicier and tastier than their mainland cousins. Growers on all the islands in Hawaii now nurture this important ingredient.

4 Moi
Once enjoyed exclusively by *ali'i* (royalty), this small, delicate fish is now on menus throughout the islands.

5 Local Fish
Myriad varieties of local fish, including *mahimahi*, *ahi*, *opakapaka*, and *onaga*, form the foundation of Hawaii cuisine.

6 Moloka'i Sweet Potatoes
With their brilliant purple flesh, these wonderful potatoes add flavor and color to dishes.

7 Corn
Chefs delight in using sweet, locally grown corn – both white and yellow corn is cultivated in the islands.

8 Slipper Lobster
Smaller than their Maine cousins; it is the sweet tail meat that is prized most.

9 Pohole
These bright green, crunchy, and delicious ferns grow in East Maui and are often served with tomatoes.

10 Local Meat
Beef, lamb, even elk and venison are produced by Hawaii ranches and used extensively by local chefs.

🔟 Honolulu and O'ahu for Free

Concert by the Royal Hawaiian Band

1 Royal Hawaiian Band Concert

MAP J3/M7 ▪ 922 5331 ▪ www.rhb-music.com

Founded in 1836, the Royal Hawaiian Band is the oldest municipal band in the US. Watch them perform Friday at noon on the grounds of the 'Iolani Palace *(see pp18–19)* and at Kapiolani Park on Sundays at 2pm.

2 US Army Museum

Housed inside Battery Randolph, an old gun battery at Waikīkī Beach, this museum displays films, artifacts, and documents relating to the military history of pre-Imperial Hawaii, World War II, the Vietnam War, and the Korean War *(see p77)*.

3 USS Arizona Memorial

Over two million visitors a year take the boat ride to this emotive World War II memorial. The short film and informative audio tour add to the humbling experience. Tickets are free but must be reserved ahead of your visit, either online for a small fee or at the on-site visitors center (the former is recommended) *(see pp12–13)*.

4 Courtyard Cinema

MAP G6 ▪ 1240 Ala Moana Blvd ▪ 369 9600 ▪ www.wardvillage.com

On the second Thursday of each month, the Hawaii International Film Festival hosts a film screening at the courtyard of the Ward Village shopping complex. There are food trucks and a cash bar, complimentary popcorn, and free parking. Tickets are free but must be reserved in advance online.

5 Royal Hawaiian Center Classes

MAP J6 ▪ 2201 Kalākaua Ave ▪ 922 2299 ▪ www.royalhawaiiancenter.com

During the week, this shopping mall offers one-hour cultural classes, including ukulele playing, *lei* making, hula dancing, and weaving. Spaces are limited and are allocated on a first-come, first-served basis.

6 Manoa Falls Trail

A 1.6-mile (2.6-km) round-trip through the misty Manoa Valley rainforest leads to a waterfall and back. The Night Marchers (spirits of ancient Hawaiian warriors) are said to haunt these historical hunting grounds. The hike is free, but the parking lot at the entrance of the trail costs $5 *(see p42)*.

Visitors at the USS Arizona Memorial

7 Farmer's Market KCC

MAP C7 ■ 4303 Diamond Head Rd ■ 848 2074 ■ Open 7:30–11am Sat ■ www.hfbf.org

Vendors gather at the Kapiolani Community College to sell flowers, vegetables, fruit, plants, coffee, honey, nuts, meat, seafood, and crafts. Parking fills up fast, so consider taking a bus instead.

8 Koko Crater Botanical Garden

Wander through a dry crater housing a significant collection of drought-tolerant, rare, and endangered plant species from Hawaii and around the world (see p29).

Cacti, Koko Crater Botanical Garden

9 The Hawaii State Art Museum

Three gallery spaces showcase unique and local fine art and craftwork, both contemporary and historical. The sculpture garden, shop, and café are splendid, too. Free hands-on art activites and entertainment for all the family make this museum particularly popular (see p17).

10 Nuuanu Petroglyphs

MAP B6 ■ 2233 Nuuanu Ave

Behind the 19th-century Nuuanu Memorial Park and Mortuary, a grassy trail leads down to a stream and three protected petroglyph sites. Etched onto large boulders centuries ago, the petroglyphs depict mostly human and dog-like figures. There are two small but pretty waterfalls along the trail as well.

TOP 10 BUDGET TIPS

1 Travel during the low seasons
Flights and accommodation prices will be at their most reasonable during April, May, September, and October.

2 Consider staying in a condo
Save money by cooking your own meals in self-catering accommodation.

3 Forgo the beachfront location
Choosing a hotel that is not directly on the waterfront (or a room without sea views) will save you money.

4 Time it right
Look for early-bird dinner specials and happy-hour offerings. *Keiki* (kids) often get discounted menu items, too.

5 Use local transportation
All-day passes for O'ahu's public transportation system cost a mere $5.

6 Swim, hike, and walk
Most beaches in O'ahu are public and free to explore, as are many hiking trails, lookouts, and parks.

7 Discover wildlife without a guide
Sea turtles, monk seals, dolphins, and whales can be spotted at places such as Lanikai Beach, Electric Beach, the Hālona Blowhole, and Makua Beach.

8 Go on a self-guided tour
Download the free map of downtown Honolulu from the Historic Hawaii Foundation (www.historichawaii.org).

9 Be entertained on Waikiki Beach
Watch free hula performances near the Duke Kahanamoku statue (6:30–7:30pm Tue, Thu, and Sat). On Friday nights, the Hilton Hawaiian Village puts on a fireworks show.

10 Eat like a local
Shop at farmers' markets and grocery stores. Food vendors offer inexpensive but delicious fare at the Eat the Street event (last Friday of every month).

Fruit stalls in Chinatown

TOP 10 Festivals

Vibrant parade celebrating Chinese New Year in Honolulu

1 Chinese New Year
Early Feb

The sound of hundreds of thousands of firecrackers, the time-honored Lion Dance, and bountiful feasts mark Chinese New Year in the islands. Anyone can take part.

2 Honolulu Festival
Mar ▪ www.honolulu festival.com

Thousands are drawn to this three-day event that celebrates the diverse cultures of the Pacific Rim. Expect to see a grand parade with performances, live music, a craft fair, food stalls, games for kids, and fireworks.

Clowns at the Honolulu Festival

3 Lei Day
May 1st

"May Day is Lei Day" are the lyrics of a popular Hawaiian song. Not that anyone in the islands needs an excuse to make, wear, or give a *lei*, but May 1st is the day when master *lei* makers showcase their skills.

4 Lantern Floating Ceremony
Last Mon in May ▪ www.lantern floatinghawaii.com

People flock to Ala Moana Beach Park each Memorial Day for the setting adrift of thousands of lanterns to remember those who lost their lives in conflict.

5 King Kamehameha Day Celebration
Jun 11th ▪ www.kamehamehaday celebration.org

The highlight of the events marking the King's birthday is O'ahu's colorful Floral Parade, which wends its way through Honolulu and Waikīkī, ending at Kapi'olani Park. Other activities include concerts, a Folklife Festival, and an international hula competition.

6 Prince Lot Hula Festival
Third Sat Jul ▪ www.moanalua gardensfoundation.org

Held at Moanalua Gardens, this is the oldest non-competitive hula event in Hawaii. It is named for Prince Lot, who reigned briefly as King Kamehameha V and was known for his commitment to perpetuation of the Hawaiian culture.

7 **Hawaii State Farm Fair**
Mid-Jul ■ www.hawaii
statefarmfair.org
Perennial favorites at this fair are the
Country Market, which sells produce
from island farms, the 4-H Livestock
Exhibition, and the Plant Sale.

8 **Hawaii Food and Wine Festival**
Early Sep ■ www.hawaiifoodand
winefestival.com
Culinary masterminds from around
the globe participate in this week-long
gastronomic festival held in Oʻahu. It
celebrates Hawaii's abundance of
seafood, beef, and poultry with wine
tastings, dinners, and special events.

Floral parade at Aloha Festivals

9 **Aloha Festivals**
Mid-Sep ■ www.aloha
festivals.com
Contemporary Hawaii is celebrated
during these festivities, which begin
on Oʻahu and move through the island
chain with at least a week-long celebration at every stop. There are floral
parades, concerts, and craft fairs.

10 **Honolulu City Lights**
Dec ■ www.honolulucity
lights.com
In early December the switch is
flipped that lights the city Christmas
tree and signals the start of the
Honolulu City Lights Electric Parade.

TOP 10 SPORTS EVENTS

1 Sony Open
This prestigious PGA tournament is
played in January at Waialae Country
Club in Honolulu.

2 Great Aloha Run
Tens of thousands run the 8-mile
(13-km) race near downtown on
President's Day (Feb), many for charity.

3 Transpacific Yacht Race
Better known simply as the Transpac,
this sees yachts race from the California
coast to Hawaii every other July.

4 Duke's OceanFest
This ocean sports competition is
held throughout Waikīkī during the
last week of August.

5 Nā Wahine O Ke Kai/Molokaʻi Hoe
First the women in late September,
then the men in mid-October paddle
outriggers across the island channels.

6 UH Sports
Locals go hog-wild over the amateur
volleyball, football, and other games
held at the University of Hawaii in winter.

7 Outrigger Rainbow Classic Basketball Tournament
A holiday tournament features the
University basketball team competing
against its mainland counterparts. It is
held at Aloha Stadium (usually Nov).

8 Vans Triple Crown of Surfing
Professional surfers from all over the
world gather on the North Shore in
November/December.

9 Hawaiʻi Bowl
Two top-ranked college football teams
compete around Christmas in sunny
Honolulu at Aloha Stadium.

10 Honolulu Marathon
In December some 25,000 international
runners enjoy Oʻahu's scenic course.

Runners at the Honolulu Marathon

Honolulu and Oʻahu Area by Area

Tranquil Hanauma Bay, home to a remarkable underwater park

🔟 Honolulu

Honolulu is often described as being noisy, overcrowded, and traffic-bound. It is all of these things, but this island capital feels far less busy than most other major US cities. Honolulu's civic role is that of state capital and seat of the City and County of Honolulu government, but, above all, it is a cosmopolitan center. Full of historic interest, the city is a great jumping-off point for all kinds of tourism, from guided walks to inter-island cruises. Downtown tends to get quiet after 5pm, but the port and Chinatown districts stay lively into the small hours.

Lei-adorned statue of Liliʻuokalani

Honolulu's Royal Mausoleum

1 Royal Mausoleum
MAP B6 ▪ 2261 Nuʻuanu Ave ▪ 536 7602 ▪ Open Mon–Fri

The mausoleum contains the bones of post-contact Hawaiian royalty except for Kamehameha Nui, who was interred in an unknown Hawaii Island location in accordance with custom, and Kamehameha II (Liholiho), whose grave is at Kawaiahaʻo. An 1865 coral chapel is the cemetery's centerpiece.

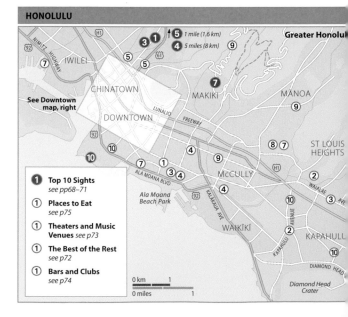

HONOLULU

Greater Honolulu

1 mile (1,6 km)
5 miles (8 km)

NIMITZ HIGHWAY
IWILEI
CHINATOWN
MAKIKI
MĀNOA
See Downtown map, right
DOWNTOWN
LUNALIO FREEWAY
ST LOUIS HEIGHTS
ALA MOANA BLVD
McCULLY
WAIALAE
Ala Moana Beach Park
KALĀKAUA AVE
WAIKĪKĪ
KAPAHULU
DIAMOND HEAD
Diamond Head Crater

1	**Top 10 Sights** see pp68–71
1	**Places to Eat** see p75
1	**Theaters and Music Venues** see p73
1	**The Best of the Rest** see p72
1	**Bars and Clubs** see p74

0 km   1
0 miles   1

2 Statue of Liliʻuokalani
MAP J3

Weighted with *lei* (garlands) and symbolism, this exceptionally life-like bronze sculpture of Hawaii's last queen stands on the south grounds of the State Capitol *(see pp16–17)*. In her hand she holds a copy of her evocative composition *Aloha ʻOe*, the 1893 Constitution, and the *Kumu Lipo*, Hawaii's creation story. *Hoʻokupu* (gift offerings) are often left here by sovereignty activists who revere this queen, who was forced to give up the monarchy under protest *(see p37)*.

3 Oʻahu Cemetery
MAP B6 ■ 2162 Nuʻuanu Ave ■ 538 1538 ■ Open 7am–6pm daily ■ www.oahucemetery.org

The gravestones of this hillside resting place founded in 1844 read like a who's who of Hawaii history, from the humble to the high-class. Nanette Napoleon, "the cemetery lady," has written a guidebook and leads periodic tours – both are well worth seeking out.

View from the Nuʻuanu Pali Lookout

4 Nuʻuanu Pali Lookout
MAP E5 ■ Off Pali Hwy

As famous for its hair-ruffling winds as for its blood-soaked history, this vantage point is where Kamehameha the Conqueror fought the final battle with Oʻahu warriors *(see p36)*. The latter either jumped to their deaths or fought until they were pushed over the cliff edge rather than give in. This atmospheric site is sometimes cold and misty, but always spectac-ular and somewhat spooky.

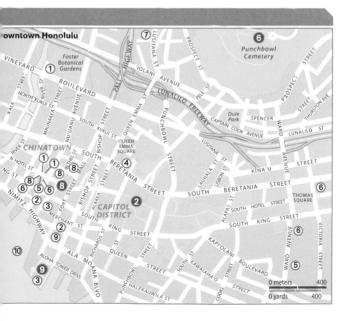

5 Queen Emma Summer Palace

MAP C5 ■ **2913 Pali Hwy** ■ **595 3167**
■ **Open 9am–4pm daily** ■ **Adm**

Hānaiakamalama, a modest white, wood-frame house with high ceilings and deep porches, was the perfect warm-weather retreat, just far enough up the Nuʻuanu Heights from Honolulu to catch chilly breezes. Queen Emma (née Rooke), who married King Kamehameha IV in 1856, inherited the home from her uncle. The palace was slated for destruction in the early 1900s, but was saved by the Daughters of Hawaiʻi organization, who now operate it as a museum.

Queen Emma Summer Palace

6 Punchbowl Cemetery

MAP L1 ■ **2177 Puowaina Dr**
■ **532 3720** ■ **Open 8am–6:30pm daily** ■ **American Legion members lead tours for a fee**

Among Oʻahu's most visited sites, the National Memorial Cemetery of the Pacific, spectacularly situated inside a volcanic crater, offers its

Aerial view of Punchbowl Cemetery

> **THE DUCK**
>
> That odd-looking, green-and-yellow vehicle that you are likely to see in downtown Honolulu is the "Duck," a World War II-vintage amphibious craft (DUKW was a manufacturer's acronym), refitted for open-air touring. Call 988 3825 to book a trip on the Duck.

visitors extraordinary views and a humbling sense of the human sacrifice brought about by the various wars in the Pacific.

7 Honolulu Museum of Art Spalding House

MAP C6 ■ **2411 Makiki Heights Dr**
■ **526 1322** ■ **Open 10am–4pm Tue–Sun** ■ **Adm (free third Sun of month)**

A gracious family property on Makiki Heights overlooking Honolulu has become a world-class art center, showcasing cutting-edge work. In addition, there are delightful gardens, a quirky gift shop, and an exceptional café.

8 Nuʻuanu Cultural District

MAP H2 ■ **Between Nimitz and Beretania, River and Bishop Sts**

Also known as Gallery Row, this vibrant area between downtown and Chinatown is a blended community of art galleries selling traditional and modern Hawaiian paintings, textiles, and glass, and restaurants, theaters, bars, and nightclubs. The best time to get a sense of its rich life is on the first Friday evening of each month, when galleries and boutiques hold

the First Friday Gallery Walk and stay open until 9pm, offering wine and *pūpū* (snacks), music, and opportunities to meet the artists.

The imposing Aloha Tower

⑨ Aloha Tower
MAP H4 ■ Pier 9, Honolulu Harbor ■ 528 5700 ■ Open 9am–9pm daily (to 6pm Sun) ■ www.aloha tower.com

This landmark building was not a success as a shopping complex, and has reinvented itself as an integral part of Hawai'i Pacific University, with residences, classrooms, restaurants, and spaces for community events. The ten-story tower, built in 1926 and standing at 184 ft (56 m), was once the tallest building in Hawaii. Today, visitors can take an elevator to the top floor for stunning views over the harbor and mountains.

⑩ Kaka'ako Waterfront Park
MAP B6

On the waterfront, between Sand Island and Ala Moana Beach Park, Kaka'ako Waterfront Park offers grassy knolls, picnic pavilions, and walking and biking paths. It also has views from 'Ewa to Diamond Head, and you can watch the surfers up close at the infamous Point Panic.

MORNING IN CHINATOWN

▶ EARLY MORNING

Chinatown is best enjoyed right after breakfast, when the stands overflow with locally grown fruits and vegetables, imported Asian goods, Pacific fish, freshly made noodles, and every possible part of the chicken and pig. Wear comfortable shoes, dress for sunshine, and park at one of the less expensive municipal lots on Smith or Maunakea Streets.

The area between River and Nu'uanu, Beretania and King is great for small gifts – sandalwood soap, painted fans, kitchen tools, dried persimmons, Chinese pottery, and red-and-gold good-luck banners. You can watch the butchers chop *char siu* (barbecue pork) with incredible speed and skill and buy some fresh fruit from one of the market stalls.

LATE MORNING

When you're ready, head *mauka* (toward the mountains) on River Street until you meet up with North Vineyard Boulevard. There you'll find the gorgeously arrayed **Kuan Yin Temple** *(see p72)* and cool, green **Foster Botanical Gardens** *(see p44)*. Explore these before returning to Chinatown for lunch.

Try one of the popular eateries in the Chinatown area, such as **Cuu Long II** (Vietnamese on N. Hotel), **Char Hung Sut** (dim sum on N. Pauahi), **Little Village Noodle House** (Chinese on Smith Street), **To Chau** (*pho* soup on River Street), or the stuffed French bread sandwiches at **Rice Paper** on Manunakea Street.

See map on pp68–9 ←

The Best of the Rest

1 Kuan Yin Temple
MAP H1 ■ 170 N. Vineyard Blvd
■ 533 6361 ■ Open daily

Light bounces off the exterior of this Chinese place of worship; inside, incense drifts and the goddess of mercy looks on as devotees pray.

Exterior of the Kuan Yin Temple

2 Alexander & Baldwin Building
MAP H3 ■ Bishop and Merchant Sts

This 1929 four-story terracotta-and-tile A&B building epitomizes Territorial period Hawaiian architecture. Asian, Mediterranean, and island influences have been combined by Hawaiian architects C.W. Dickey and Hart Wood.

3 Ala Moana Center
MAP B6 ■ 1450 Ala Moana Blvd
■ 955 9517

With more than 350 stores and regular live entertainment, this is Hawaii's largest shopping mall its and most visited destination.

4 Ala Wai Canal
MAP G5–M6, G6

With a wide path along its entire length, the canal offers a lovely evening's walk, ending at the Ala Wai Yacht Harbor.

5 Liliʻuokalani Botanical Gardens
MAP B6 ■ North Kuakini St, Honolulu
■ 522 7060

This garden was a retreat for the queen. It is said that she picnicked to the tinkling sounds of Nuʻuanu Stream *(see p45)*.

6 Academy Art Center
1111 Victoria St ■ 532 8741

This center sees exhibitions and sales of various art societies. The work on offer is often very affordable.

7 TEMARI Center for Asian and Pacific Arts
MAP K2 ■ 1754 Lusitana St (Hongpa Hongwanji Temple) ■ 536 4566

This art group was founded when a few crafters met in 1979 to share their knowledge of Asian arts. Now the center hosts prestigious classes.

8 University of Hawaiʻi
Info from Campus Center: 956 7235 ■ www.hawaii.edu

Two self-guided walking tours focus on the campus's plant life and art work.

9 Tantalus Drive
MAP E5

The loop drive from Makiki Street up Round Top Drive, and along Tantalus Drive is not to be missed – picnic along the way at Puʻu ʻUalakaʻa Park.

10 Honolulu Harbor
MAP G3–H3

Almost all of the state's waterborne traffic passes through here, and 98 percent of imports are brought to the islands by water. A great spot from which to watch harbor life is the patio of Gordon Biersch *(see p74)*.

Skyline around the Honolulu Harbor

Theaters and Music Venues

A Motown tribute act at The Republik

1 The Republik
MAP M4 ■ 1349 Kapiolani Blvd ■ 941 7469

This trendy event space hosts an array of performers, from international DJs and 80s bands to tribute acts. Under-18s require an adult to accompany them to the concert hall. Its adjoining lounge, The Safehouse, serves great food and drinks.

2 Mamiya Theatre
3142 Wai'alae Ave ■ 739 4886

Mamiya, named for the pioneering heart surgeon who funded it, is a space used for recitals, dance, and performances.

3 Kumu Kahua
MAP H3 ■ 46 Merchant St ■ 536 4441

This 100-seat experimental theater focuses on new cutting-edge work from around the Pacific.

4 Tenney Theatre
MAP J2 ■ 229 Queen Emma Sq ■ 838 9885

The Tenney is a small performance center that hosts the Hawaiian Theatre for Youth.

5 Neal S. Blaisdell Arena
MAP L3 ■ 777 Ward Ave ■ 591 2211

When Honolulu lands a rock show or traveling circus, this basic hall is where it happens.

6 Neal S. Blaisdell Concert Hall
MAP L3 ■ 777 Ward Ave ■ 591 2211

The 2,185-seat Neal S. Blaisdell Concert Hall is home to the Honolulu Symphony, the Hawaii Opera Theatre, Ballet Hawaii's annual holiday *Nutcracker*, and most other symphonic events.

7 Kennedy Theatre
1770 East-West Rd, UH campus ■ 956 7655

The campus theater has a 600-seat main theater and the smaller Earle Ernst Lab Theatre. The season includes plays and musicals, and Kabuki and Noh Japanese dramas.

8 Hawaii Theatre Center
MAP H2 ■ 1130 Bethel St ■ Box office: 528 0506

A former movie theater, the wonderfully renovated Hawaii Theatre Center offers a full and varied season, from *hula hālau* fundraisers to visiting dance companies.

The Hawaii Theatre Center at night

9 Manoa Valley Theatre
2833 E. Mānoa Rd ■ 988 6131

This small but highly respected theater in a former church hall stages plays and musicals.

10 Diamond Head Theatre
520 Makapu'u Ave, Kaimukī ■ 733 0274

A varied program, from beloved musicals to pidgin English fairy tales, and comedy to contemporary drama, is offered at this community theater.

See map on pp68–9

Bars and Clubs

1 **Manifest**
MAP H2 ■ 32 N. Hotel St
■ 645 0763

Modern coffee shop by day, and trendy lounge by night, this Chinatown hangout is a favorite see-and-be-seen spot among the city's sophisticates.

2 **Murphy's Bar and Grill**
MAP H3 ■ 2 Merchant St
■ 531 0422

Downtown watering hole that offers a taste of Ireland; it also hosts one of the Pacific's largest St. Patrick's Day celebrations.

3 **Gordon Biersch**
MAP H4 ■ Aloha Tower Marketplace ■ 599 4877

The pier-side bar becomes a club on weekends – one of the few where you can dance outdoors. There's occasional live music, which tends towards contemporary rock.

4 **Mai Tai Bar**
MAP B6 ■ Ala Moana Shopping Center ■ 947 2900

Very much a local favorite, this bar has live Jawaiian (local reggae) music, comfortable couches, and a relaxed lounge style.

5 **Smith's Union Bar**
MAP H2 ■ 19 N. Hotel St
■ 538 9145

A down-and-dirty dive bar that has been serving cheap drinks to a wide mix of customers since 1935. It hosts karaoke every night.

6 **The Dragon Upstairs**
MAP H2 ■ 1038 Nu'uanu Ave
■ 526 1411

Some of the city's top jazz musicians gather at this intimate Chinatown hideaway to jam through the night, much to the delight of music lovers.

7 **Ryan's Grill**
MAP B6 ■ Ward Center, 1200 Ala Moana Blvd ■ 591 9132

Munch your way through the delicious *pūpū* (snacks) menu at this place and be mesmerized by the colored bottles in the backbar.

8 **The Tchin Tchin! Bar**
MAP H2 ■ 39 N. Hotel St
■ 528 1888

Visit on the first Friday of the month (for First Friday Art Gallery Walk), and this wine and cocktail bar, along with all the other bars in this part of Chinatown, will be full of jovial locals.

9 **Bar Leather Apron**
MAP H3 ■ 745 Fort St
■ 524 0808

This stylish speakeasy whisky bar offers creative, well-balanced concoctions. Score one of the six seats at the bar for top-notch service.

10 **Moku Kitchen**
MAP G5 ■ 145-660 Ala Moana Blvd ■ 591 6658

A modern, urban restaurant, Moku Kitchen gets lively in the evenings with music. It has more than 36 craft beers, plus 12 biodynamic wines on tap. Happy hour runs from 3pm to 5:30pm.

Band jamming at the Mai Tai Bar

Places to Eat

1 **Lucky Belly**
MAP H2 ■ 50 N. Hotel St
■ 531 1888 ■ $

It's not just the ramen that draws a nightly crowd to this Chinatown joint. Try the equally tempting oxtail dumplings and the *kochujang* brisket *bibimbap (see p60)*.

2 **Uncle Bo's**
MAP M7 ■ 559 Kapahulu Ave ■ 735 8311 ■ $$

Uncle Bo's is one of Waikīkī's most popular late-night spots for wildly creative appetizers and social snacks. The modern, casual environs attract a hip clientele.

3 **Town**
MAP C7 ■ 3435 Waiale'e Ave ■ 735 5900 ■ $$

This trendy, youthful eatery in Kaimukī is nationally acclaimed for its commitment to local and organic ingredients *(see p60)*.

4 **Sushi Sasabune**
MAP B6 ■ 1417 S. King St ■ 947 3800 ■ $$$

The *omakase* menu here is justly famous, with perfectly seasoned bites, from oysters to octopus to abalone, scallops, *ahi*, and more. Reservations are a must at this superb venue.

5 **Burgers and Things**
MAP E5 ■ 1991 Pauoa Rd, Honolulu ■ 971 1946 ■ $

A plain-looking eatery, Burgers and Things is known for its braised burgers and huge sandwiches piled high with meat and fresh vegetables.

6 **The Pig and the Lady**
MAP J3 ■ 83 N. King St
■ 585 8255 ■ $$

Traditional family recipes combined with innovative cooking skills make up the Vietnamese dishes enjoyed at communal tables here *(see p61)*.

7 **Nico's Pier 38**
MAP H3 ■ 1129 N. Nimitz Hwy
■ 540 1377 ■ $$$

Lyon-born chef Nico Chaize creates gourmet dishes using market-fresh fish in a relaxing waterfront location with indoor and outdoor seating. There is also a bar and a fish market.

Whole fried fish with a tomato salad

8 **Rain Honolulu**
MAP H3 ■ 1138 Fort St Mall
■ 200 0910 ■ $$

Daily drinks specials, happy hours, and innovative takes on old favorites, such as pulled pork nachos, make this a popular restaurant.

9 **Alan Wong's Restaurant**
MAP H3 ■ 1857 S. King St
■ 949 2526 ■ $$$

European style is married with the best island cooking techniques at one of Hawaii's top restaurants *(see p60)*.

10 **Leonard's Bakery**
MAP M7 ■ 933 Kapahulu Ave
■ 737 5591 ■ $

Founded in 1952, this beloved local bakery specializes in *malassadas* (Portuguese doughnuts).

See map on pp68 9 ←

ᴛᴏᴘ10 Waikīkī

Waikīkī, the famous resort area containing the most sought-after real estate in Hawaii, is a vibrant neighborhood, with world-class shopping, restaurants, entertainment venues, and numerous hotels. The International Market Place is more popular than ever; the grassy walks along Waikīkī Beach bloom with plantings; statuary commemorates historic figures; and the Kapiʻolani Park Bandstand regularly hosts concerts. All the more reason the inhabitants say, *"E komo mai!,"* or *"Welcome!,"* to visitors.

Sun-seekers on palm-lined Kūhiō Beach Park

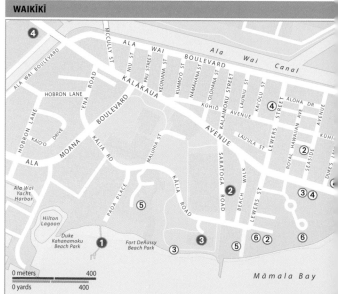

WAIKĪKĪ

Mamala Bay

| 0 meters | 400 |
| 0 yards | 400 |

1 Atlantis Submarines Waikiki

MAP H7 ■ 252 Paoa Pl ■ 973 9800
■ Open 9am–4pm daily ■ www.
atlantisadventures.com

Those who want to venture under
water to view sea life without all
the gear and training can join an eco-
tour via an authentic submarine. Air-
conditioned vessels dive to depths
of up to 100 ft
(30 m). Through
large windows, you
can see green sea
turtles, stingrays,
sharks, yellow
tangs, and other
underwater
marine life.

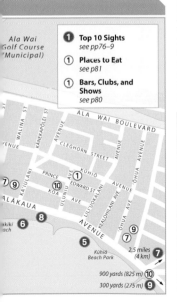

Tank in the US Army Museum

2 Urasenke Tea House

MAP J6 ■ 245 Saratoga Rd
■ 923 3059 ■ Donation

Teaching Cha-do, the Way of Tea, a
ceremony meant to both relax and
focus the mind, is the mission of this
center endowed by the Urasenke
Foundation in Kyoto. Public

demonstrations are offered weekly,
and private ones can be arranged
by calling ahead.

3 US Army Museum

MAP J7 ■ Battery Randolph,
Kālia Rd, Fort DeRussy ■ 438 2825
■ Open 10am–5pm Tue–Sat
■ www.hiarmymuseumsoc.org

This well-designed free
museum celebrates
the US Army's many-
faceted history in
the Pacific. It
covers Hawaii's
"Go for Broke"
100th Infantry
Battalion, Waikīkī
as a Vietnam
War R&R center,
and more (see p62).

4 Hawaii Convention Center

MAP G5 ■ 1801 Kalākaua Ave.
■ 943 3500 for tour info
■ Open 8am–5pm weekdays
■ www.hawaiiconvention.com

A contemporary masterpiece of
glass and soaring white columns,
the Convention Center, across the
Ala Wai bridge from Waikīkī proper,
was dedicated in 1998 and contains
dozens of artworks and more than
a million square feet of meeting
space. The venue hosts an array of
events and performances including
the Hawaii Pops and the Hawaii Food
and Wine Festival.

The Hawaii Convention Center

WAIKĪKĪ MAGIC

At the far western end of Waikīkī is Magic Island, a man-made green peninsula lined with walkways and ending in a sandy lagoon and rock wall popular with fishermen. End the day here, watching the soft light fall and the canoe teams ready for the next regatta. Keep an eye open for the "green flash" at sunset. Parking is free.

⑤ Kūhiō Beach Park
MAP L7

Once known as Hamohamo, this area was the location of Pualeilani, the beach home of Queen Kapiʻolani and later her adopted son, Prince Jonah Kūhiō Kalanianaʻole, a delegate to the US Congress. During his lifetime he opened the beach near his home to the public, and left it to the city when he died.

View from the Diamond Head Crater

⑦ Diamond Head Crater
MAP C7 ■ Open 6am–6pm daily (last entrance 4:30pm) ■ Adm ■ Walking tour 9am Sat (free); 948 3299

Watching over Waikīkī, Diamond Head Crater's sculpted slopes are shadowy green in rainy season and a dusty parched brown at other times. In addition to the trail within the crater, a 3-mile (1.5-km) loop walk allows you to see the changeable peak from a full circle. Start where Monsarrat Avenue meets Diamond Head Road and proceed in either direction.

⑧ Kahuna (Wizard) Stones
MAP L7 ■ Kūhiō Beach, Kalākaua Ave

The four misshapen slabs at Kūhiō Beach represent four mysterious historical figures called *Kapaemahu* ("people of a changeable nature"). These men came to Hawaii from abroad and lived with the islanders, curing and educating them. The stones were erected in their memory and have occupied various locations, but are currently gathered at the beach formerly known as Ulukou.

Surf tables for rent at Waikīkī Beach

⑥ Waikīkī Beach
MAP L7

This unassuming strip of white sand covered with half-clothed bodies, surfboard racks, and gawking tourists is what Waikīkī Beach is all about. You might think only visitors use it, but you'll see surfers, daily exercisers, canoe clubs, and other locals enjoying Hawaii's best-known beach, too. Dawn and dusk are ideal times to visit *(see p49)*.

⑨ Kapiʻolani Bandstand
MAP C7 ■ Kapiʻolani Park

The current, vaguely Victorian stone structure – a spacious circular stage

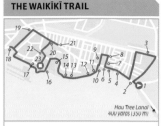

with a peaked roof held up by a series of pillars – is the fourth incarnation of a bandstand first built in the 1880s. It is a popular venue for concerts and is often used for informal jam sessions.

⑩ International Market Place

MAP K6 ■ **2330 Kalākaua Ave** ■ **Open 10am–10pm daily** ■ **www. internationalmarketplacewaikiki.com**
First opened in 1956, International Market Place reopened as a modern shopping, dining, and entertainment center in 2016 after extensive renovations. Free festivities, perfor- mances, and myriad artisan stalls ensure that even the youngest shopper is kept entertained.

Stalls at the International Market Place

THE WAIKĪKĪ TRAIL

Hau Tree Lanai
400 yards (350 m)

▶ MORNING

Take a self-guided tour along the Waikīkī Historic Trail that is maintained by the Native Hawaiian Hospitality Association. Be sure to stop at each historic trail marker to learn about the area's rich history. Visit the trail website *(www.waikikihistorictrail. org)* for a free trail map.

The trail was the brainchild of the late visionary George S. Kanahele, a pioneer of cultural tourism. It's marked by a series of sculpted surfboards imprinted with photographs, maps, and information at 23 locations around the neighborhood.

Most hikers begin at the first marker on Waikīkī Beach at the site of the Outrigger Canoe Club, founded in 1908 to promote surfing, canoe paddling, and other activities.

Stopping points include a former residence of Queen Liliʻuokalani; the villa of Chun Afong, who was Hawaii's first Chinese millionaire; the vast coconut grove of Helumoa; and a war camp of Kamehameha I.

LATE MORNING

The tour lasts about an hour- and-a-half, after which you have plenty of time to stroll some more or do some shopping.

Stop for lunch at the **Hau Tree Lanai** *(see p81)* in the Kaimana Beach Hotel at the east end of Waikīkī. Here you can sit at the exact spot where Robert Louis Stevenson enjoyed the shade under the hau tree in 1893 as he penned stories about the South Pacific.

See map on pp76–7 ⬅

Bars, Clubs, and Shows

Colorful dining room under a bamboo-and-grass roof at Duke's Waikīkī

1 Duke's Waikīkī
MAP K7 ▪ Outrigger Waikīkī on the Beach, 2335 Kalākaua Ave ▪ 922 2268

Named after surf legend Duke Kahanamoku and outfitted with his memorabilia, this popular bar offers food and live music.

2 Lewers Lounge
MAP J7 ▪ Halekulani Hotel, 2199 Kālia Rd ▪ 923 2311

This romantic cocktail lounge has some of the island's leading mixologists and features nightly live jazz.

3 KOA Oasis Booze Shack
MAP H6 ▪ Hale Koa Hotel, 2131 Kālia Rd ▪ 955 0555

Sink your toes into the soft sand with an expensive, delicious mai tai in hand at this beachfront shack.

4 Rock-A-Hula
MAP K6 ▪ Royal Hawaiian Center, 2201 Kalākaua Ave ▪ 629 7469

Tribute artists and local talent stage highly entertaining shows in a 750-seat theater. Options include pre-show drink and dinner add-ons.

5 Sharkey's Comedy Club
MAP J6 ▪ Hale Koa Hotel, 2055 Kālia Rd ▪ 531 4242

Live comedy shows, featuring both local and touring comedians, provide an affordable opportunity to laugh at the "lighter side" of the islands. Luau and magic shows are also held here.

6 RumFire
MAP K7 ▪ Sheraton Waikiki, 2255 Kalākaua Ave ▪ 922 4422

This oceanfront lounge has fire pits, live music, and cocktails. Try the Spiked Tea Experience (1–4pm daily).

7 Fourever Fab Show
MAP K7 ▪ Sheraton Princess Kaʻiulani Hotel, 120 Kaʻiulani Ave ▪ 277 8443

A must for any Beatles fan, this show features their songs played by four seasoned musicians.

8 Magic of Polynesia
MAP K7 ▪ Holiday Inn Waikīkī Beachcomber, 2300 Kalākaua Ave ▪ 971 4321

Illusionist John Hirokawa combines Polynesian culture with magic (an understudy performs on Sunday and Monday nights).

9 Te Moana Nui-Tales of the Pacific
MAP K7 ▪ Sheraton Princess Kaʻiulani, ʻAinahau Showroom, 120 Kaʻiulani Ave ▪ 921 4600 ▪ Sun, Wed & Fri

Tales of Pacific Islands and their peoples are performed through song and dance in this colorful show.

10 Wang Chung's
MAP L6 ▪ 2424 Koa Ave ▪ 921 9176

This gay-friendly nightclub, a popular karaoke spot, has specialty liquors for those in need of Dutch courage.

Places to Eat

1 **Me Bar-B-Q**
MAP L7 ■ 151 Uluniu Ave
■ 926 9717 ■ $

Visit this Korean take-out counter for tender barbecued meats, rice, and vegetables – perfect for a picnic at the beach.

2 **Heavenly**
MAP K6 ■ Shoreline Hotel Waikiki, 342 Seaside Ave ■ 923 1100 ■ $

Fresh island fruit, honey, and farm eggs are just some of the healthy local ingredients that make up the menu at this brunch diner.

3 **Doraku Sushi**
MAP K6 ■ Royal Hawaiian Center, 2233 Kalākaua Ave ■ 922 3323 ■ $$

Don't let the mall location deter you from visiting this excellent sushi hot-spot with a terrace. Good happy hour.

4 **Mahina & Sun's**
MAP K6 ■ Surfjack Hotel, 412 Lewers St ■ 924 5810 ■ $$

Chef Ed Kenney elevates Hawaiian cooking, with dishes such as octopus with watercress, and rigatoni with wild boar *(see pp60–61)*.

5 **La Mer**
MAP J7 ■ Halekulani Hotel, 2199 Kālia Rd ■ 923 2311 ■ Open dinner only ■ Jacket required ■ $$$

Savor each bite while watching the sun set at this French gourmet restaurant *(see p61)*.

> **PRICE CATEGORIES**
> Price categories include a three-course meal for one, a glass of house wine, and all unavoidable extra charges including tax.
> ....
> $ under $30 $$ $30–$60 $$$ over $60

6 **House Without a Key**
MAP J7 ■ Halekulani Hotel, 2199 Kālia Rd ■ 923 2311 ■ $$

Named after a novel featuring fictional detective Charlie Chan, this hotel hangout is a sunset favorite for cocktails or casual meals. There is also live music and hula dancing.

7 **DK Steak House**
MAP K7 ■ Waikiki Beach Marriott Resort & Spa, 2552 Kalākaua Ave ■ 931 6280 ■ $$

The steaks and seafood are outstanding here, as are sides such as truffle mac and cheese *(see p61)*.

8 **Hula Grill Waikīkī**
MAP K6 ■ 2335 Kalākaua Ave ■ 923 4852 ■ Open breakfast, lunch & dinner ■ $$

Regional Hawaiian fare is served along the water's edge, with views of the beach and Diamond Head.

9 **Sansei Seafood Restaurant & Sushi Bar**
MAP K7 ■ Waikiki Beach Marriott Resort & Spa, 2552 Kalākaua Ave ■ 931 6286 ■ $$

Come during happy hour and reserve a spot on the beach-side balcony to enjoy the Japanese fare served here *(see p60)*.

10 **Hau Tree Lanai**
MAP M7 ■ New Otani Kaimana Beach Hotel, 2863 Kalākaua Ave ■ 921 7066 ■ $$

Reasonably priced Pacific Rim cuisine is served here beneath the spreading branches of a hau tree.

The sleek, elegant entrance of La Mer

See map on pp76–7 ←

⑩ North Shore

The North Shore is many things to many people. For big-wave riders, it is the peak of their craft. For Honoluluans, it's the far, far country, and turning-around point for Sunday drives. And for those who appreciate flavorful food, it's an important source of superb produce – from tropical fruits and coffee to corn and free-range beef. The coastline itself displays a split personality over the course of the year. From April to October, the beaches are playgrounds, broad and golden, visited by gentle waves. From October to April, however, high surf robs them of sand, or piles it high into dunes, and the potential danger of swimming here cannot be overstated.

Surfing at Banzai Pipeline

① Banzai Pipeline
MAP C1

At 'Ehukai Beach Park, located between Ke Waena and Ke Nui Roads off Kamehameha Highway, expanses of sand fringe a rocky shore, over which the surf boils. The most famous of the wild surfing breaks is the tubular Banzai Pipeline. Lifeguards are kept very busy here because of the steeply sloping ocean bottom and the irresistible allure of huge winter surf (see p43).

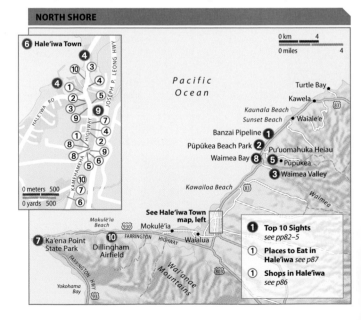

NORTH SHORE

⑥ Hale'iwa Town

Pacific Ocean

Turtle Bay
Kawela

Kaunala Beach
Sunset Beach • Waiale'e

Banzai Pipeline ①
Pūpūkea Beach Park ②   Pu'uomahuka Heiau
Waimea Bay ⑧   ⑤ • Pūpūkea
                    ③ Waimea Valley

Kawailoa Beach

See Hale'iwa Town map, left

Mokulē'ia Beach
Mokulē'ia
Waialua

⑦ Ka'ena Point State Park   ⑩ Dillingham Airfield

Yokohama Bay

Wai'anae Mountains

①	**Top 10 Sights** see pp82–5
①	**Places to Eat in Hale'iwa** see p87
①	**Shops in Hale'iwa** see p86

0 km   4
0 miles   4

0 meters   500
0 yards   500

Pūpūkea Beach Park, a popular spot for snorkelers and scuba divers

② Pūpūkea Beach Park
MAP B1

The 80 acres (32 ha) of Pūpūkea Beach Park include two very popular snorkeling and skin-diving areas. Shark's Cove is a rocky inlet, often used by scuba-diving operators for training. Three Tables is a network of shallow coral reefs and ponds. The Pūpūkea Foodland store, across the highway, is great for provisions, and the Sunset Beach Fire Station offers aid and information.

③ Waimea Valley
MAP C2 ■ 59–864
Kamehameha Hwy, Hale'iwa
■ 638 7766 ■ Open daily ■ Adm
■ www.waimeavalley.net

Once an adventure park with tram rides and cliff divers, this valley is now owned by the Office of Hawaiian Affairs. The center's focus is on the conservation of the valley's natural resources and layered history through interpretive hikes and cultural activities.

④ Hale'iwa Ali'i Beach Park and Hale'iwa Beach County Park
MAP B2

These parks flank each other on either side of the Anahulu River, and if they look familiar it's because they were a primary set for *Baywatch Hawaii*. Ali'i Park features a boat ramp and is popular for fishing and surfing *(see p48)*. Across the river, Hale'iwa Beach offers safe swimming and is an excellent place for a family party or picnic.

⑤ Pu'uomahuka Heiau
MAP C1 ■ From Kamehameha Hwy, drive up the hill on Pūpūkea Rd; the dirt track into the *luakini heiau* is on the right and is marked by a visitor attraction sign

This *luakini heiau* (sacrificial temple), honoring the war god Kū, is the largest on O'ahu. It encompasses an expansive network of three enclosures that command panoramic views of Waimea Bay and the surrounding countryside. An altar has been restored at which you may see (but not touch) personal offerings.

The historic site of Pu'uomahuka Heiau

THE WILD NORTH SHORE

If you're interested in wildlife, several beaches along this coast serve as basking areas for turtles. Wedge-tailed shearwaters nest in the area during the late summer and fall, and whales can be seen frolicking offshore between the months of November and April.

6 Haleʻiwa Town
MAP B2

Allow a couple of hours to explore historic Haleʻiwa Town, with its eclectic community of surfers, artists, and families who have lived in "the house of the ʻiwa bird" for generations. Once a gracious retreat for wealthy summer visitors, Haleʻiwa Town has a certain timelessness. To get a feel for it, park at either end of town and simply walk around admiring the plantation-era buildings, browsing the shops

Sign for Haleʻiwa Town

and art galleries, and lingering on the Anahulu River Bridge to watch the water flow by.

7 Kaʻena Point State Park
MAP A2

This sprawling state park begins at the abrupt and muddy end of Farrington Highway and takes you along a wild, boulder-strewn shore-line to the dunes at Oʻahu's western-most tip. This is said to be where the souls of the dead leapt into the afterlife. It's an extremely hot two-hour hike (Kaʻena means "the heat"), but worth it for the beauty of the landscape and the whales you can spot in season. Take sunscreen, a hat, water, and sturdy walking shoes.

8 Waimea Bay
MAP B1

This legendary surf spot *(see p50)* is also a good choice for scuba divers and free divers. It has a wide, sandy beach, which is great for sunbathing. Picnic areas, showers, and rest rooms make Waimea Bay an ideal place to spend the day. In summer the waves subside, and it is possible to swim in the ocean. However, it is important to heed lifeguard warnings. As this is one of the most popular beaches on the North Shore, parking is limited, so get there early.

Golden sand at Waimea Bay

⑨ Lili'uokalani Protestant Church

MAP B2 ■ 66–90 Kamehameha Hwy ■ 637 9364 ■ Open daily

Queen Lili'uokalani was part of this congregation when she visited her summer home in Hale'iwa. Though the present structure dates only from 1961, a century-old moon-phase clock she gave to the church is proudly displayed. The church is famed for its annual fundraising *lū'au* feast each August.

Lili'uokolani Protestant Church

⑩ Dillingham Airfield

MAP A2 ■ 69–000 Farrington Hwy, Mokulē'ia ■ 637 4551 ■ Honolulu Soaring: 637 0207; offers daily flights

This tiny airport is well known as a center for gliding, skydiving, and scenic flights *(see p52)*.

NORTH SHORE EXCURSION

▶ MORNING

A 50-mile (80-km) round trip from Waikīkī may not seem that far, but most of the route is on two-lane highways, so you can't rush, and there's a lot to see. As it is a bit too far to drive in one day, it may be worth checking in at Kahuku's **Turtle Bay Resort** *(see pp116–17)*, which offers hotel rooms and suites renovated in Plantation style, as well as condos and cottages with full kitchens and multiple bedrooms.

From there, you can easily drive into **Hale'iwa Town** for a morning's shopping – some items are cheaper than in the city, notably pareau wraps. Have lunch at **Kua'aina Sandwich Shop** or Joe's **Seafood Grill** *(see p87)*.

AFTERNOON

For the rest of the afternoon, you can keep going north and take a heart-thrilling glider ride at **Dillingham Airfield** or rent a water bicycle from **Surf N Sea** *(see p86)* in Hale'iwa Town. Alternatively, head back toward the Turtle Bay Resort, stopping to enjoy a bit of sunbathing or snorkeling along the way.

Try to plan your excursion around an event – check the Go Hawaii site *(www.gohawaii.com)* for an events calendar in advance of your trip. Highly recommended are the Toro Nagashi lantern ceremony, hosted by Hale'iwa Shingon Mission every August, and, of course, the thrilling winter championship surf meets, which aren't always easy to schedule because they are wave-dependent.

See map on p82 ⬅

Shops in Haleʻiwa

1 Haleʻiwa Art Gallery
66–252 Kamehameha Hwy
637 3368

George Atkins's gallery has works by over 30 Pacific Island artists, ranging from the Neo-Realism of Mark Cross to the abstracts of Mihoko M.

2 The Growing Keiki

66–051 Kamehameha Hwy
637 4544

For unique, handmade items for kids, check out the eclectic array of funky clothing, books, toys, and gifts at this children's shop.

3 San Lorenzo Bikinis
66-057 Kamehameha Hwy
637 3200

This store sells a unique assortment of bikinis, some with daringly cheeky designs. You can mix and match them. They also have beach hats and towels.

4 Rainbow Bridge Gift Shop
62–620 Kamehameha Hwy
637 7770

Choose from colorful sarongs, beach towels, ukuleles, and locally made shirts and jewelry, all at fair prices, at this lovely gift shop.

5 Polynesian Treasures
North Shore Marketplace
637 1288

Stacked with unusual designs by more than 50 artisans, handicrafts shop has carved bone amulets and quilted items.

6 Silver Moon Emporium

North Shore Marketplace
637 7710

You'll think you're in SoHo or Hollywood when you step into this ritzy boutique packed with designer clothes and shoes of the wispy, whimsical type. This is where the movie, TV, and sports stars shop when they visit the North Shore.

7 North Shore Surf Shop

66–200 Kamehameha Hwy
637 6777

Surfing gear, clothing, snacks, rentals, and lessons are offered here by friendly surfers who are keen and familiar with the area. They can tell you where the best waves are.

8 Barnfield's Raging Isle Surf and Cycle

North Shore Marketplace 637 7707

This store has everything for bicycles, including rentals and repairs. You'll also find custom boards by Bill Barnfield and stylish casual wear.

9 Mahina
66–111 Kamehameha Hwy
784 0909

A wonderful collection of breezy sundresses, light tops, and trousers in soft fabrics, plus a range of coordinating accessories, is available at this women's clothing store.

10 Surf N Sea
62–595 Kamehameha Hwy
637 9887

Established in 1965, this watersports-fanatics' paradise is the oldest surf shop on Oʻahu. It offers everything from swimwear to snorkel tours and kayak rentals. The friendly staff will even fix that ding in your board after you've tackled Waimea Bay.

The venerable Surf N Sea shop

Places to Eat in Hale'iwa

PRICE CATEGORIES

Price categories include a three-course meal for one, a glass of house wine, and all unavoidable extra charges including tax.

$ under $30 $$ $30–$60 $$$ over $60

1 Hale'iwa Joe's Seafood Grill
66–011 Kamehameha Hwy
■ 637 8005 ■ $$

With a view of Hale'iwa harbor from its patio, this friendly open-air restaurant specializes in "boat drinks" and fresh fish.

2 Waialua Bakery
66–200 Kamehameha Hwy
■ 637 9079 ■ $

The excellent smoothies, sandwiches, and cookies keep visitors coming back for more at this bakery, popular with surfers.

3 Hale'iwa Beach House
62–540 Kamehameha Hwy
■ 637 3435 ■ $$

Classic Hawaiian seafood dishes, *pupu* platters, and colorful cocktails are served in this airy spot on the beach.

4 Kua'aina Sandwich Shop
60–160 Kamehameha Hwy
■ 637 6067 ■ $

This fast-food eatery is famous for its good-value third-of-a-pound burgers and crisp fries. It also serves gourmet sandwiches and salads.

5 Shave Ice Stops
Matsumoto's (66–087 K. Hwy)
■ **Aoki's (66–082 K. Hwy)**

Two neighboring operations offer sweet, drippy shave ice, a legacy of the days when ice was shipped to Hawai'i from Alaska in giant blocks. The shavings, created when the blocks were cut, were treasured by children. In the 1920s, Chinese entrepreneurs made fruit syrups to pour over the ice, and Japanese craftsmen created a plane-like device to shave it. Pick the shortest line and enjoy.

6 Surf N Salsa
66–521 Kamehameha Hwy
■ 692 2471 ■ $

Stop by this popular food truck for fresh Mexican food that can be picked up and eaten here or savored at a shaded picnic table.

7 Giovanni's Shrimp Truck
66–472 Kamehameha Hwy
■ 293 1839 ■ $

This food truck serves large plates of ridiculously good (if unpeeled) garlic shrimp. Be aware of the long lines.

Crowds at Giovanni's Shrimp Truck

8 Kono's
67–250 Kamehameha Hwy
■ 637 9211 ■ $

Try the breakfast bomber burrito or 12-hour braised pork plate, both top picks at this breakfast/brunch spot.

9 Coffee Gallery
North Shore Marketplace
■ 637 5571 ■ $

Locally grown coffees are roasted daily at this internet café. The specialty espresso drinks are popular.

10 Café Hale'iwa
66–460 Kamehameha Hwy
■ 637 5516 ■ $

Mexican-accented lunches preceded by ample breakfasts are the fare at this café, which is open only until mid-afternoon. A popular surfer hangout, it's good for people-watching and for finding out what's on in town.

See map on p82

TOP 10 Central and Leeward Oʻahu

If you have the time to venture beyond the glamour of Waikīkī and the allure of the North Shore, Central and Leeward Oʻahu offer the chance to better understand the everyday life of the island – the neighborhoods and shops, the down-home restaurants, and the lesser-known beaches. ʻEwa, once the quintessential company town, recalls its roots with a reconstruction plantation village. Ko Olina's gentle lagoons and the beaches of Waiʻanae offer great sun and sand time. Several sacred sites – some restored, some mere remnants – remind us of the historical importance of these areas.

Outrigger canoes on the sandy beach at tranquil Pōkaʻi Bay

CENTRAL AND LEEWARD OʻAHU

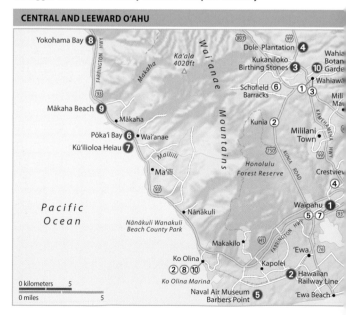

Previous pages The Diamond Head crater seen from Waikīkī Beach

Room at Hawaii's Plantation Village

as Hawaiians, labored on sugar and pineapple plantations is memorialized in the 30 original structures gathered to create this living history museum. Tours are led by volunteers, many of whom are former plantation laborers or descendants of workers.

② Hawaiian Railway Line

MAP C5 ■ Catch the train from 91–1001 Renton Rd, ʻEwa ■ 681 5461 ■ Open 3pm Sat, 1pm & 3pm Sun ■ Adm ■ www.hawaiianrailway.com

The Hawaiian Railway Line consists of six restored miles of what were once 70-plus miles (113 km) of track delivering people and supplies from ʻEwa to Honolulu. A service operates only on weekends, offering 90-minute round trips to the coast at Ko Olina and back. Take the train, and then later drive back to Ko Olina to swim in the man-made lagoons in the shade of coco-palms. You can also have lunch or dinner at the JW Marriott ʻIhilani Resort & Spa.

① Hawaii's Plantation Village

MAP C4 ■ 94–695 Waipahu St, Waipahu ■ 677 0110 ■ Open 10am–3pm Mon–Sat ■ Adm age 4+ ■ www.hawaiiplantationvillage.org

The era when more than 400,000 immigrants from China, Japan, Korea, and the Philippines, as well

③ Kukaniloko Birthing Stones

MAP C3 ■ From Kamehameha Hwy heading toward Wahiawā, turn left on Whitmore Rd, then continue to the dirt parking lot and the palm grove

Bloodlines were all-important to ancient Hawaiians. In royal birthing areas like Kukaniloko, the upright stones served as support for the chiefly mother and also as chairs for the attendant priests and relatives, on hand to testify to the child's royal lineage.

Top 10 Sights
see pp90–93

① Places to Eat
see p95

① The Best of the Rest
see p94

The birthing stones at Kukaniloko

Dining al fresco under the parasols of the Dole Plantation's patio

4 Dole Plantation
MAP C3 ▪ 64–1550 Kamehameha Hwy ▪ 621 8408 ▪ Open 9am–5:30pm daily ▪ www.dole-plantation.com

The gardens and production facilities of this attraction introduce 900,000 visitors a year to Oʻahu's modern-day diversified agriculture industry. As well as pineapples, growing here are coffee, tropical fruit, corn, *lei* flowers, and exotic bromeliads. The Pineapple Garden maze, officially recognized in the Guinness Book of Records as the world's largest maze, offers an unusual diversion.

5 Naval Air Museum Barbers Point
MAP B5 ▪ Kalaeloa Airport, 91–1299A Midway St, Kapolei ▪ 682 3982 ▪ Open Tue–Sun by appt ▪ Adm ▪ www.nambp.org

This former army base now houses a museum where visitors can view up close over a dozen aircraft and even the interiors of several cockpits. The museum is located on an active airport, so visits are by guided tour only and need to be pre-arranged.

6 Pōkaʻi Bay
MAP A4 ▪ 5–037 Waiʻanae Valley Rd

Beautiful, tranquil Pōkaʻi Beach County Park is the most welcoming swimming and snorkeling beach along the Waiʻanae Coast. It's safe all year round because of the protection of a long breakwater. The bay's name, "night of the great one," is rooted in the story of a voyager from the south, Pōkaʻi, who is said to have planted the first coconut grove on the island on this site.

7 Kūʻilioloa Heiau
MAP A4

This sacred site on Kāneʻilio Point is believed to have been a blessing point for travelers arriving and departing by canoe. Its name refers to a dog-god who protected voyagers.

KAʻENA FROM THE WEST

Though most folks come to Kaʻena Point from the Mokulēʻia side, the 5-mile (8-km) trek from the Waiʻanae direction offers a sandier section of the old Farrington Highway. En route, watch for yellow *ʻilima*, purple *pāʻū o hiʻiaka*, and white *naupaka* flowers.

8 Yokohama Bay
MAP A3

So-called because of its popularity with Japanese pole fishermen, this is the last sandy shore on the northwestern coast of Oʻahu. It's also part of a large but undeveloped park complex that stretches around the end of the island to Kaʻena. Though known as a popular surfing site, it is also a place where you can enjoy the beach in relative isolation.

9 Mākaha Beach
MAP A3 ■ 84–369 Farrington Hwy

Mākaha (meaning "fierce") lives up to its name, with high surf and a runoff pond behind the beach that periodically breaks through the sand bar and rushes into the bay. In the past, it was infamous for a group of bandits who terrorized the area. Today, with the exception of when the surf is high, it is a safe beach for swimming.

The high surf at Mākaha Beach

10 Wahiawā Botanical Gardens
MAP C3 ■ 1396 California Ave, Wahiawā ■ 621 5463 ■ Open 9am–4pm daily ■ Guided tours available

Founded by commercial sugar planters as an experimental arboretum in the 1920s, this rainforest garden has tropical flora that require a cooler climate. The emphasis is on native Hawaiian plants, although there are also many plants from other countries around the world. Many of the older trees date to the 1920s (see p45).

A DAY WITH DOLPHINS

MORNING

Schools of spinner and bottlenose dolphins, and, from November to March, pods of humpback whales are readily seen just off the Waiʻanae Coast. Several cruise companies offer dolphin-watching excursions in various craft, usually with small numbers of passengers. The excursions depart from **Waiʻanae Boat Harbor** or **Ko Olina Marina**. Most offer transport from Waikīkī hotels, though you can choose to pick up the tour at the harbor. You will have to get up early, though, because the boats usually depart promptly at 7am.

Wild Side Specialty Tours (306 7273, www.sailhawaii.com) offers a whale- and dolphin-watching cruise aboard a 42-ft (13-m) catamaran. It is operated by marine researchers who believe that sail-powered vessels are less disruptive to the animals. The boat accommodates an intimate 4 to 15 passengers, and all the four-hour morning excursions include refreshments.

AFTERNOON

After your cruise, head over to **Monkeypod Kitchen** (see p95) for lunch – if you time your meal to finish around 3:30pm, you will then be able to catch the happy hour and live-music segment.

Spend the rest of the afternoon watching the green sea turtles at nearby **Paradise Cove Beach**. This is a quiet, pretty spot and it's good for small children, but be aware that there are no lifeguards. Later, go for dinner and drinks at **Ko Olina Resort** (92–1089 Alii Nui Drive).

See map on pp90–91

The Best of the Rest

Tiki masks, Aloha Stadium Swap Meet

1 Aloha Stadium Swap Meet

MAP D4 ■ 99–500 Salt Lake Blvd ■ 486 6704 ■ Open 8am–3pm Wed & Sat, 6:30am–3pm Sun

Ringed around the stadium, the largest swap meet in the islands is a great place for kitsch souvenirs, alohawear, and beach equipment.

2 Manulele Distillers

MAP C3 ■ 92–1770 Kunia Rd, Kunia ■ 649 0830 ■ Open 10am–5pm daily ■ www.kohanarum.com

Find out how the rum for your mai tai is made on a one-hour tour that includes tastings and a souvenir glass to take home.

3 Wahiawā Town

MAP C3

Primarily a military town, dusty Wahiawā, high on the central plain, is a useful stop-off for supplies when journeying through the hinterland.

4 Waikele Premium Outlets

MAP C4 ■ 94–790 Lumiana St, Waipahu, Exit 5A off H1 ■ 676 5656

More than 50 outlet stores, including Sak's Fifth Avenue, Coach, Banana Republic, Calvin Klein, Levi's, and Tommy Hilfiger, feature at this mall.

5 Waipahu Town

MAP C4

This one-time plantation town is the hub for O'ahu's Filipino community. Activities at the large Filcom Center (94–428 Mokuola St) include dance and martial-arts classes and film screenings.

6 Tropic Lightning Museum

MAP B3 ■ Schofield Barracks (request entry at Lyman Gate and bring photo ID) ■ 808 655 0438 ■ Open 10am–4pm Tue–Sat

Housing memorabilia from the US 25th Infantry Division (nicknamed "Tropic Lightning"), this museum helps to explain the American military history of O'ahu .

7 Don Quijote

MAP C4 ■ 94–144 Farrington Hwy, Waipahu ■ 678 6800

Open 24 hours, this Japanese discount store makes for a convenient stop for groceries, inexpensive souvenirs, and other essentials.

8 Pearlridge Shopping Center

MAP D4 ■ 98–1005 Moanalua Rd, 'Aiea ■ 488 0981

This shopping mall is comprised of two main sections linked by a monorail. It is especially popular with tweens and teens.

9 'Aiea Bowl

MAP D4 ■ 99–115 'Aiea Heights Dr ■ 488 6854

A family-friendly spot by day, this bustling bowling alley also has many dining options. Things liven up at night, with glow-in-the-dark "cosmic bowling" and dancing until 2am.

10 Ice Palace

MAP D5 ■ 4510 Salt Lake Blvd ■ 487 9921 ■ Adm

O'ahu's full service ice rink is open daily for public skating and is a perfect escape from the heat.

Places to Eat

1 **Sunnyside**
MAP C3 ▪ 1017 Kilani Ave, Wahiawā ▪ 621 4858 ▪ $

This popular breakfast spot serves island specialties such as fried rice with hot dogs, fresh fruit, and cream pies. Expect long lines on weekends.

2 **Monkeypod Kitchen**
MAP B5 ▪ 92–1048 Olani St, Kapolei ▪ 380 4086 ▪ $$

Listen to live music while enjoying farm-to-table Hawaiian food and views of the surrounding golf course.

3 **Buzz's Original Steak House, 'Aiea**
MAP D4 ▪ 98–751 Kuahou Pl, 'Aiea, Pearl City ▪ 487 6465 ▪ $$

A longtime local favorite, Buzz's is known for its generous salad bar, grilled steaks, and fresh seafood. The original "Original" is in Kailua.

Sliced barbecue striploin steak

4 **Shiro's Saimin Haven & Family Restaurant**
MAP D5 ▪ Waimalu Shopping Center, 98–020 Kamehameha Hwy, 'Aiea ▪ 488 8824 ▪ $

This shrine to Japanese-style noodle soup and plate lunches has to be seen to be believed. Founder Shiro Matsuo has lined the walls with notes expressing his philosophy of life.

5 **Anna Miller's**
MAP D4 ▪ 98–115 Kaonohi St, 'Aiea ▪ 487 2421 ▪ $

Renowned for its homemade pies and friendly staff, this popular

PRICE CATEGORIES
Price categories include a three-course meal for one, a glass of house wine, and all unavoidable extra charges including tax.

$ under $30 $$ $30–$60 $$$ over $60

family restaurant will serve you breakfast, lunch, or dinner 24 hours a day.

6 **Boston's North End Pizza Bakery**
MAP D4 ▪ 98–298 Kamehameha Hwy, 'Aiea ▪ 487 4055 ▪ $

The pies are Boston-style – thick edge, thin center, cheesy, saucy – and the attitude is East Coast too. That means "eat it and beat it."

7 **Restaurant 604**
MAP D4 ▪ 57 Arizona Memorial Dr, Honolulu ▪ 888 7616 ▪ $$

Live music and great views feature at this friendly, open-air marina-side pub. Try the Kalua pork nachos.

8 **Roy's Ko Olina**
MAP B5 ▪ 92–110 Aliinui Dr, Ko Olina Golf Club ▪ 676 7697 ▪ $$

Award-winning restaurateur and chef Roy Yamaguchi perfects his Hawaii fusion cuisine, while bringing the excitement of his open-plan kitchen to the islands.

9 **Ichiriki**
MAP D4 ▪ 98–150 Kaonohi St, 'Aiea ▪ 484 2222 ▪ $$

At this restaurant specializing in savory *nabe* (Japanese hot pot), you get to choose the broth, vegetables, seafood, meat, and noodles. Then you cook it yourself.

10 **'Ama 'Ama**
MAP B5 ▪ Aulani Resort, 92–1185 Ali'inui Dr, Ko Olina ▪ 674 6200 ▪ $$

Disney's most lauded restaurant serves modern interpretations of classic Hawaiian dishes in a scenic beachfront setting.

See map on pp90–91 ←

TOP 10 Windward O'ahu

Going from Kailua to Kahuku means traveling from town to country. Kailua, a bedroom community of Honolulu, is an upscale neighborhood of beach and lake homes, while Kāne'ohe accommodates a Marine base and Hawaiian homesteads. North from Kāne'ohe, the route along Kamehameha Highway passes a string of sandy beaches and brooding valleys, watched over by the Ko'olau Mountain Range.

Kayaking to the Ahu o Laka Sandbar

1 Ahu o Laka Sandbar
MAP E3

At low tide on a weekend, drive slowly on Kamehameha Highway just past He'eia Kea Boat Harbor. A little way offshore, you'll see watercraft of every description clustered around seemingly nothing at all. In fact, just above sea level is a sandbar, and locals like to gather here, light the hibachi and hang out.

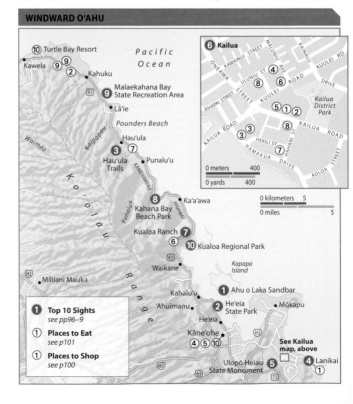

WINDWARD O'AHU

10 Turtle Bay Resort
Kawela 9 9
2 Kahuku
Malaekahana Bay State Recreation Area
9
Lā'ie
Pounders Beach
Hau'ula
3 7
Hau'ula Punalu'u
Trails
8 Ka'a'awa
Kahana Bay Beach Park
Kualoa Ranch 7
6 10 Kualoa Regional Park
Waikane
Mililani Mauka
Kahalu'u
'Ahuimanu
He'eia
Kāne'ohe
4 5 10
Ulopō Heiau State Monument

Pacific Ocean

6 Kailua
ONEAWA
KAWAINUI STREET
MALUNIU AVE
KANALU
ULUNIU ST
KUULEI RD
8 6 ROAD
DRIVE
KIHAPAI STREET STREET
KUULEI STREET
Kailua District Park
5 1 2
KAILUA ROAD
3 KAILUA ROAD
8
3
HEKILI ST
7
HAMAKUA DRIVE
AOLOA STREET
0 meters 400
0 yards 400

0 kilometers 5
0 miles 5

Kapapa Island

1 Ahu o Laka Sandbar
2 He'eia State Park • Mōkapu

See Kailua map, above

4 Lanikai
1

K o ' o l a u   R a n g e

Waimea
Koʻlopapau
Punaluʻu
KAMEHAMEHA HIGHWAY
H2
H3
63
72

1 Top 10 Sights
see pp96–9

1 Places to Eat
see p101

1 Places to Shop
see p100

2 Heʻeia State Park and Fishponds

Surrounded by mangrove swamp, this grassy, well-maintained state park *(see p31)* is located on Kāneʻohe Bay, which contains Oʻahu's only barrier reef. The park offers a view of the long Heʻeia fishpond, the largest intact aquaculture zone in the islands. There are several other fishponds in the vicinity. When in use, fingerlings of the prized *ʻamaʻama* (mullet) and *ʻahole* (Hawaiian flagtail) swim into the rock-walled ponds through vertical gates called *mākaha*, but are unable to swim out. In this way, the fish are successfully farmed.

3 Hauʻula Trails

MAP D2 ▪ From Kamehameha (Hwy 83), the trails are reached by Hauʻula Homestead Rd and Maʻakua Rd

Hauʻula ("red *hau* tree" in Hawaiian) is the starting point for three very good rambles that range from easy to moderate (a fourth hike, Sacred Falls, is closed indefinitely due to landslide danger). The two most worthwhile treks are Maʻakua Loop and Maʻakua Ridge (aka Papali Trail); both offer good views, interesting plants, and guavas in their late summer and fall season.

4 Lanikai

MAP F4

Developed as a beach retreat in the 1920s, beautiful Lanikai (which is

reached by a beach road south of Kailua) remains one of the most sought-after addresses on the island of Oʻahu. This tight-knit neighborhood hosts community plays and an exceptional pre-Christmas craft fair.

Ancient temple at Ulupō Heiau

5 Ulupō Heiau State Monument

MAP E4

Some locals still visit this historic location to arrange leaf-wrapped gift bundles on the massive rock platform, formerly a site of prayer, sacrifice, ceremony, and divination. Likely built during the time of Kamehameha I, the *heiau* continued in use until the ancient religion was officially abandoned. To find it, head toward Kailua on Highway 61, turn left into Uluʻoa Street at the Windward YMCA, park in the Y lot or along the street and follow the signs.

Sun-worshipers relaxing on beautiful Lanikai beach

6 Kailua
MAP F4

This country-chic town consists of a few blocks of shops and restaurants, peaceful 1960s-era neighborhoods, and a string of popular beaches (see p49). Park along Kailua Road and explore on foot, weaving in and out of interesting gift and clothing shops. At No. 600, Lanikai Juice serves delicious smoothies and juices.

Open-air shopping mall at Kailua

7 Kualoa Ranch
MAP E3 ■ Kualoa Ranch & Activity Club, 49–560 Kamehameha Hwy ■ 237 7321

The valley and rolling hillsides of Kualoa were once a sacred place of refuge, then passed to missionary descendants from royal hands. Today, Kualoa is a working cattle ranch, as well as a park where visitors can enjoy equestrian experiences and movie tours (see p47). The ranch is a popular filming spot, appearing in movies and TV shows such as *Jurassic Park* and *Lost*.

Cattle on the green pastures of Kualoa Ranch

SHRIMP TRUCKS

Northbound on Kamehameha Highway between Kāne'ohe and Kahuku, you'll encounter a string of shrimp trucks, some in lunchwagons, others in roadside stands. It all began with a single shrimp aquaculture operation, which sparked a North Shore love affair with crustaceans. If you stop, be sure to ask if the shrimp you're buying are locally grown (some aren't) or previously frozen.

8 Kahana Bay Beach Park/Kahana Valley
MAP D2 ■ Kualoa Ranch & Activity Club, Kamehameha Hwy ■ 237 7321

State-owned watershed land, the deep Kahana Valley is fronted by an 8-acre (3-ha) city and county park. The park has a sandy beach, bathrooms, picnic tables, a large number of chickens (escaped fowl are ubiquitous all along this coast), and the remnants of two fishponds. Watch for fishermen wading out to catch *akule* (big-eyed scad).

9 Malaekahana Bay State Recreation Area
MAP D1

This curving sandy beach is distinguished by bare-bones beach homes available for rent, a reef that keeps the inshore waters calm, and Goat Island, a wild and beautiful place that can be reached on foot at low tide; be sure to wear beach shoes, though, or you may cut your feet on the reef.

Chinaman's Hat seen from Kualoa Park

⑩ Kualoa Regional Park
MAP E3

The flat, windy Kualoa Regional Park features a narrow sandy beach and shallow inshore ponds. It is a fantastic spot for activities such as kite-flying, snorkeling, launching watercraft, picnicking, and camping (by permit). The clearly visible peak sitting on the ocean (sometimes known across the island as the Chinaman's Hat) is the island of Mokoli'i (see p30), popular with kayakers.

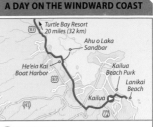

▶ MORNING

Begin your itinerary by heading straight for **Kailua**, where you can stop off at Agnes Bake Shop (46 Ho'olai St) for coffee and malassadas (Portuguese dough-nuts, freshly made and eaten hot).

Treat yourself to some Hawaiian scents and lotions at Lanikai Bath and Body (600 Kailua Rd). If you're feeling peckish, pick up an authentic plate lunch at Fatboy's Local Drive-In (301A Hahani St) for a true taste of the island.

Then head for **Kailua Beach Park** (see p49) or **Lanikai Beach** (see p49) for the afternoon. Either is good for surfing, swimming, snorkeling, and boating.

AFTERNOON

You could opt for a sun-soaked lazy afternoon, but if you fancy a little more activity, rent some form of watercraft from Bob Twogood Kayaks (www.twogood kayaks.com) or from Kailua Sailboards and Kayaks (www. kailuasailboards.com). Then, either paddle out to the **Nā Mokulua** islets (see p49) off Kailua Beach or drive over to **He'eia Kai Boat Harbor** and head to the **Ahu o Laka Sandbar** (see p96).

If you do plan to spend more time on the coast, consider reserving one of the luxurious rooms at the **Turtle Bay Resort** (see pp116–17). You can loiter your way from Kailua to Kahuku, leaving mid-afternoon and making one or two stops, and still arrive by check-in time. You won't have to face the long drive back across the island, and you can dine in the extra-ordinary **Pa'akai** restaurant (p101).

See map on p96 ←

Places to Shop

1 Under a Hula Moon
MAP F4 ▪ 600 Kailua Rd, Kailua Shopping Center ▪ 261 4252

A delightful, Hawaiian-themed gift shop, Under a Hula Moon sells clothes, home accessories, jewelry, and artworks.

2 Bookends in Kailua
MAP F4 ▪ 600 Kailua Rd, Kailua Shopping Center ▪ 261 1996

This bookstore is run by readers for readers and has comfy chairs and a mix of new and used books, stacked high. It has a good children's section.

3 Foodland
MAP F4 ▪ 108 Hekili St, Kailua ▪ 261 3211

The area's largest supermarket stocks almost everything – from snacks and health supplies to local produce such as macadamia nuts.

4 Manoa Chocolate Hawaii
MAP F4 ▪ 203–315 Uluniu St, Kailua ▪ 262 6789

Most of the ingredients in the chocolate bars at this small shop and factory are sourced in Hawaii. They also offer tasting tours.

5 Island Treasures Art Gallery
MAP F4 ▪ 629 Kailua Rd, Kailua Shopping Center ▪ 261 8131

Kailua Koa wood craft, *lauhala* (woven pandanus) creations, and ceramics are among the treasures for sale here. They are mostly made by local artists.

Inside the Island Treasures Art Gallery

6 Kailua General Store
MAP F4 ▪ 316 Kuulei Rd, Kailua ▪ 261 5740

Island artworks, local honey, clothes, natural soaps, handmade gift items, and refreshing shave ice can be found at this friendly concept store.

7 Kim Taylor Reece Gallery
MAP D2 ▪ 53–866 Kamehameha Hwy, Hau'ula ▪ 293 2000 ▪ Open Mon–Wed afternoons only

Reece's photographs portray alluring hula dancers in traditional dress. Hand-printed sepia originals, posters, and Reece's books are all available.

8 Global Village
MAP F4 ▪ 539 Kailua Rd, Kailua ▪ 262 8183

Originally a bead store, this family-owned business now also sells clothing for children and adults, jewelry, gifts, and accessories. It also holds bead workshops.

9 Only Show in Town
MAP D1 ▪ 56–901 Kamehameha Hwy, Kahuku ▪ 293 1295

Antiques and collectibles from all eras in Hawaiian history, as well as from a beguiling miscellany of other times and places, are available here.

10 Kanile'a Ukulele
MAP E4 ▪ 46–216 Kahuhipa St, Kāne'ohe ▪ 234 2868 ▪ Factory tours 10:30am Mon–Fri

This is one of the best places to purchase an authentic, locally made ukulele. Lessons are available, too.

Places to Eat

PRICE CATEGORIES

Price categories include a three-course meal for one, a glass of house wine, and all unavoidable extra charges including tax.

$ under $30 $$ $30–$60 $$$ over $60

1 Buzz's Original Steak House

MAP F4 ■ 413 Kawailoa Rd, Lanikai ■ 261 4661 ■ $$

This venerable spot – a warren of dim rooms scented with the delicious aroma of grilling meat – serves surf and turf to a broad clientele from Lanikai millionaires to sandy surfers.

2 Kahaku Farm Cafe

MAP C1 ■ 56–800 Kamehameha Hwy, Kahuku ■ 293 8159 ■ $

Most of the vegetarian items here are made with freshly picked fruit and vegetables from the 5-acre (2-ha) family farm. Try the banana bread and the Tropi-kale smoothie.

3 Prima Hawaii

MAP F4 ■ 108 Hekili St, Kailua ■ 888 8933 ■ $$

A modern Italian/American restaurant, Prima Hawaii uses fresh, local meat and produce in its dishes. The Kiawe wood-fired brick oven pizza is a favorite.

4 Haleiwa Joe's

MAP E4 ■ 46–336 Ha'ikū Rd, Kāne'ohe ■ 247 6671 ■ $$

Call to check Joe's isn't reserved for a wedding – neighboring Ha'ikū Gardens does a booming bride-and-groom business. If open, expect steaks, seafood, and sandwiches.

5 Pah Ke's Chinese Restaurant

MAP E4 ■ 46–018 Kamehameha Hwy, Kāne'ohe ■ 235 4505 ■ $

As well as the chop suey standards, Pah Ke's specials include chilled fruit soups and dishes that focus on locally grown tropical fruits.

6 Aunty Pat's Paniolo Café

MAP E3 ■ Kualoa Ranch, 49–560 Kamehameha Hwy ■ 237 7321 ■ $

Named for a descendant of the Kualoa Ranch's founder, this casual café serves breakfasts and lunches, including gourmet burgers made fresh from the ranch's herd.

Burger and fries – a popular meal

7 Boots & Kimo's Homestyle Kitchen

MAP F4 ■ 151 Hekili St, Kailua ■ 263 7929 ■ $

Popular with locals and tourists, this welcoming café often has lengthy lines for its delicious macadamia nut pancakes and Portuguese sausage.

8 Uahi Island Grill

MAP F4 ■ 33 Aulike St, Kailua ■ 266 4646 ■ $

This casual local institution serves contemporary island favorites as well as traditional plate lunches.

9 Hi-BBQ

MAP C1 ■ 66–540 Kamehameha Hwy, Haleiwa ■ 724 2341 ■ $

Fall-off-the-bone American-style barbecued meats are on offer at this mountaintop food truck with views of the shrimp farms and ocean below.

10 Pa'akai

MAP C1 ■ 57–091 Kamehameha Hwy, Turtle Bay Resort ■ 293 6000 ■ $$

The name Pa'akai means "sea salt" in the Hawaiian language. Enjoy sea-to-table fare, which features local, organic ingredients.

See map on p96 ←

TOP 10 South Shore

It's an easy drive around the South Shore of Oʻahu from Waikīkī to the rural village of Waimānalo, but over those 12 miles (19 km), you experience the island's multidimensional nature. After the exclusive community of Kāhala, you come to a series of densely populated valley neighborhoods. Each of these climbs from a coral-fringed beach to the apex of a deep valley in the classic Hawaiian land division known as an *ahupuaʻa*. At the island's edge, the coast provides an ecologically fragile landscape, before giving way to mile upon mile of golden sand, bordering the horse country.

Admiring the view from a rocky outcrop at Makapuʻu Beach Park

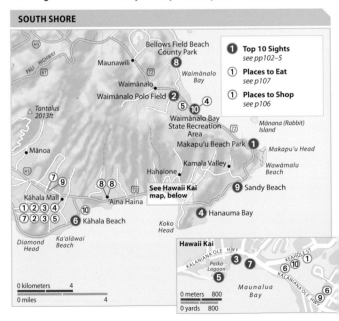

SOUTH SHORE

1 **Top 10 Sights**
see pp102–5

1 **Places to Eat**
see p107

1 **Places to Shop**
see p106

1 Makapuʻu Beach Park
MAP F5

This park contains some of Oʻahu's most beloved landmarks – the beach (a bodysurfer's mecca; see p50), the nearby lighthouse, and the shore trail. Just over the rocks lies "baby beach," where shallow tide pools are safe for young children to splash around in. Manana, better known as Rabbit Island, is a dramatic landmark standing offshore.

2 Waimānalo Polo Field
Honolulu Polo Club: MAP F5; matches 3pm Sun Jun–Oct; adm, under 16s and military personnel free with ID; www.honolulupolo.org

Polo, a sport favored by Hawaiian royalty, boasts a 200-year history in the islands. Spread across 27 green acres (11 ha), the Honolulu Polo Club offers a shaded grandstand, food for sale, and plenty of *aloha* (warmth) for visitors. Past guests have included the UK's Prince Charles, who played a match here in 1974.

3 Kuliʻouʻou Beach Park
MAP F6

This family-friendly beach park on Maunalua Bay offers a number of picnic sites, scenic views, and, at low tide, the opportunity for novice kayakers to take to the water. To get there, from Kalanianaʻole, turn right onto Kuliʻouʻou Road, left onto Summer Street and right again onto Bay Street, which shortly comes to a dead end in the parking lot.

Small, idyllic beach at Hanauma Bay

4 Hanauma Bay
MAP F6

Keyhole-shaped Hanauma Bay is one of the most spectacular sights in the islands, and highly recommended for swimming and snorkeling. It's a good idea to go early in the day because the bay is so well used that access and parking can be difficult. Call ahead on 396 4229 to check for periodic closures.

5 Paikō Lagoon State Reserve
MAP F5

The virtually unknown Paikō Peninsula (its name derives from a Portuguese former resident called Pico) offers birdwatching, fishing, snorkeling, and unprecedented seclusion. From Kalanianaʻole, turn right onto narrow Paikō Drive, park on the street and take the beach access trail to the water. Turn left (east) and find your spot past the second to last house. Bring food and water with you, as it's a remote area.

Canoes at Kuliʻouʻou Beach Park

The breathtaking landscape surrounding Kāhala Beach

6 Kāhala Beach
MAP E6

This remote stretch of golden sand, hidden by suburban Kāhala's ritzy homes, offers snorkeling, reef-fishing, and sunbathing. To get here from Waikīkī, take Diamond Head Road until it becomes Kāhala Avenue. In the 4,400 to 4,800 blocks of Kāhala Avenue, watch out for seven narrow paths, marked by blue beach access signs (park on the street). The bigger stretch of Waiʻalae Beach Park is just beyond Kapakahi Stream bridge.

On a canoe in Maunalua Bay

7 Maunalua Bay Beach Park
MAP F6

This sun-baked park has picnic tables, restrooms, and some grassy areas for play. It's a launching point for excursions onto Maunalua Bay, from outrigger canoe paddling and water-skiing to fishing, diving, and snorkeling trips.

8 Bellows Field Beach County Park
MAP F4 ■ Camping by permit only

Although located on a military installation (which includes an army reserve camp where Marines practice amphibious landings), this sprawling beach and campsite with ample parking is a public facility on weekends and holidays. Many consider it the best of the Waimānalo beaches; bodyboarding, boogieboarding, and surfing are prime (see p48).

9 Sandy Beach
MAP F5

Renowned for the constant winds that make kite-flying a feature and for the surf that breaks very near to its shore, Sandy Beach is very popular with bodyboarders and surfers. Great caution should be taken as the waves routinely slam unsuspecting waders into the

---

KITE FLYING

On any suitably windy day at Sandy Beach, the sky is bright with colorful kites. Flyers from the ages of 6 to 60 play out the lines, straining against the wind. Traditionally, Hawaiian kites were made from hau wood, covered with kappa or woven lauhala, with olonā cord used for the string. Skill was needed both to make and fly them.

rock-hard sand. Don't turn your back on the ocean – here, or anywhere else (see p51).

⑩ Waimānalo Bay State Recreation Area
MAP F5

Here you catch sight of uninterrupted white sand that stretches 3 miles (5 km) along the coast. The facility includes Waimānalo Beach Park to the south, and the recreation area to the north. Both offer prime picnic areas, campsites, restrooms, and showers. The park is on the road but the recreation area is secluded in an ironwood grove (known as Sherwood Forest, in part because car burglaries are a problem).

Lifeguard hut at Waimānalo Beach

SOUTH SHORE TOUR

▶ MORNING

A South Shore circular driving tour makes for a great all-day itinerary. Starting from **Waikīkī**, pick up breakfast pastries from Fendu Boulangerie in **Manoa Marketplace** (Woodlawn Drive via University Ave).

Head back down south, take the H1 east, and finish off the morning with a water adventure, such as water-skiing or diving, at **Maunalua Bay**. Reserve ahead at water activity shops at Hawaii Kai Towne Center or Koko Marina Center. For a more sedate pursuit, take binoculars and go bird-watching on the edge of the **Paikō Lagoon State Reserve** (see p103).

Back on Kalaniana'ole, grab a quick lunch at **Kona Brewing Co.** (see p107) or one of a dozen inexpensive, interesting eateries at **Koko Marina Center** (see p106).

AFTERNOON

Cruise slowly around the island's edge, stopping to view the **Hālona Blow Hole** (see p43) and watch the bodysurfers and kite-fliers at **Sandy Beach**. November through May the Blow Hole is a vantage point to see whales migrating.

At **Makapu'u Wayside**, park and make the easy hour-long, 2-mile (3-km) trek up and down the old lighthouse road; the views will stay with you for a long time.

Afterwards, stop for a drink or a bite to eat at the **Hawaiian Island Café** (see p107) and enjoy a refreshing swim at **Waimānalo Beach** before heading home via the Pali Highway.

See map on p102 ←

Places to Shop

Browsing inside Whole Foods Market

1 Whole Foods Market
MAP E6 ▪ Kāhala Mall, 4211 Waiʻalae Ave, 2000 ▪ 738 0820

This widely popular, mainland chain is a one-stop store for an array of locally produced food and gift items. It stocks an extensive range of bakery products, cheese, and beverages, including beer and wine, as well as poultry and seafood.

2 33 Butterflies
MAP E6 ▪ Kahala Mall, 4211 Waiʻalae Ave ▪ 380 8585

The chic, on-trend women's clothing here features a wide range of styles.

3 Vue Hawaii
MAP E6 ▪ Kāhala Mall, 4211 Waiʻalae Ave ▪ 735 8774

Many of the island-themed gifts at this shop are handmade in Hawaii by local artisans.

4 Paperie
MAP E6 ▪ Kāhala Mall, 4211 Waiʻalae Ave ▪ 735 6464

The Paperie is chock full of fine-quality paper goods such as Hawaii-themed cards, stationery, and wedding supplies.

5 Roadside Stands
MAP F5

Watch for charming roadside stands near Waimānalo. They sell fresh kahuku corn, fruits, chilled coconuts, tropical flowers, fresh or dried fish, and such ethnic specialties as pasteles (Puerto Rican tamales) and poke (raw fish and seaweed salad).

6 Koko Marina Center
MAP F6 ▪ 7192 Kalanianaʻole Hwy ▪ 395 4737

This shopping center includes a vast supermarket, theater complex, many eateries, and places to rent water gear or arrange excursions along the coast.

7 The Compleat Kitchen
MAP E6 ▪ Kāhala Mall, 4211 Waiʻalae Ave ▪ 737 5827

Honolulu's first upscale kitchen supply store stocks gorgeous bamboo cutting boards and other high-quality gifts for foodies.

8 ʻAina Haina Shopping Center
MAP E5 ▪ 820–850 W. Hind Dr, Honolulu ▪ 732 7736

Anchored by the local grocery chain Foodland Farms, this modern strip mall is great for local goodies including Hawaii's special apple bananas and fresh tuna poke.

9 Gecko Books & Comics
MAP E6 ▪ 1151, 12th Ave, Honolulu ▪ 732 1292

A treasure trove of rare, hard-to-find comics, as well as toys, games, and trading cards, are sure to appeal to the child in everyone at this tiny family-owned shop.

10 Hawaii Kai Towne Center and Hawaii Kai Shopping Center
MAP F5 ▪ Towne Center: 6700 Kalanianaʻole Hwy; 396 0766 ▪ Shopping Center: 377 Keahole; 395 1018

These side-by-side open malls offer grocery shopping, dive shops, boat charter firms, and restaurants, as well as banks and dry-cleaners.

See map on p102

Places to Eat

PRICE CATEGORIES
Price categories include a three-course meal for one, a glass of house wine, and all unavoidable extra charges including tax.

$ under $30 $$ $30–60 $$$ over $60

1 Island Brew Coffeehouse
MAP F5 ▪ 377 Keahole St, Honolulu ▪ 394 8770 ▪ $

Healthy sandwich bagels, acai bowls, and 100 percent Hawaiian coffee are served at this simple breakfast and lunch spot. There is a beautiful view over the water from the back patio.

2 The Counter
MAP E6 ▪ Kāhala Mall, 4211 Wai'alae Ave ▪ 739 5100 ▪ $

You can build your own burger here, or try one of the signature offerings: the Loco Moco combines a ground beef patty, fried egg, onion strings, and gravy on a bed of rice.

3 Olive Tree Café
MAP E6 ▪ 4614 Kīlauea Ave, Kaimuki ▪ 737 0303 ▪ $

One of the few Mediterranean restaurants in the islands, this spot routinely wins awards for its great Greek fare and casual style.

4 Hawaiian Island Café
MAP F5 ▪ 41–865 Kalaniana'ole Hwy, Waimanalo ▪ 808 200 4637 ▪ $

This friendly, cozy spot specializes in huge sandwiches, pizzas, and fresh juices, all made with local organic ingredients.

5 Zippy's
MAP E6 ▪ 4134 Wai'alae Ave, Kāhala ▪ 733 3730 ▪ $

This seaside outpost of one of the island's most popular chains serves inexpensive, island-style comfort food (hamburger curry, won ton noodle soup) and house signature chili.

6 Roy's Restaurant
MAP F5 ▪ 6600 Kalaniana'ole Hwy, Hawaii Kai ▪ 396 7697 ▪ $$

The flagship of the sprawling Roy's Restaurant empire continues to deliver its trademarks: high-energy atmosphere, a dramatic open-plan kitchen, and a menu that ranges from salsa to Szechuan (see p61).

7 Koko Head Café
MAP C7 ▪ 1145c 12th Ave, Honolulu ▪ 732 8920 ▪ $

Locals head to this divine brunch diner for a Pan-Asian twist on breakfast classics. Expect a line and take some kimchi bacon cheddar scones home (see p60).

8 Jack's Restaurant
MAP E5 ▪ 'Aina Haina Shopping Center, 820 W. Hind ▪ 373 4034 ▪ $

Stop by this compact neighborhood spot to discover Jack's giant Special Biscuits and freshly made local plates. Breakfast is served until 2pm.

9 Kona Brewing Co.
MAP F6 ▪ Koko Marina Center, 7192 Kalaniana'ole Hwy ▪ 394 5662 ▪ $

The first O'ahu brewpub by Big Island-based Kona Brewing, located on one of Hawaii Kai's man-made canals, serves burgers, salads, casual fare, and, of course, beer.

10 Plumeria Beach House
MAP E6 ▪ Kāhala Hotel & Resort, 5000 Kāhala Ave ▪ 739 8760 ▪ $$

This oceanfront, indoor/outdoor restaurant is family-friendly and well known for lavish buffets.

Patio at Plumeria Beach House

Streetsmart

Brightly colored surfboards in front of the ocean

Getting To and Around Honolulu and Oʻahu

Arriving by Air

Honolulu International Airport (HNL), located 9 miles (14 km) northwest of Waikīkī, is one of the busiest airports in the US. Most major domestic and international airlines fly to HNL, including **American Airlines, Alaska Airlines, Qantas, Air New Zealand, Air Canada**, and **WestJet**.

The complimentary Wiki-Wiki Bus shuttles between HNL's three terminals and the gates. Information booths can be found in the Baggage Claim area and outside the Foreign Arrivals area.

Contrary to what you may see in old movies, *lei* greeters do not welcome every new arrival. If, however, you are on a package tour, you will likely be greeted with a *lei* and a peck on the cheek from a company employee. If you're visiting friends or family, you will surely receive a garland upon arrival.

After the Baggage Claim area, there will be shuttles and taxis (look for the yellow Taxi Dispatcher for service) to take you to your hotel. A one-way taxi trip to Waikīkī costs about $40. Shuttles cost about $16 per passenger to Waikīkī.

If you are renting a car, six rental companies have registration counters in the Baggage Claim area. Several other car-rental companies have off-site lots, and their vans are waiting outside on ground level to pick passengers up. If you are traveling really light (your baggage must fit under the seat), **TheBus**, the island's public transportation system, is the cheapest option, at $2.50 for a one-way fare to Waikīkī. Take either the No. 19 or No. 20 bus.

Arriving by Sea

Numerous cruise lines have Oʻahu on their itinerary, arriving mostly during the winter months. They dock at either of the two cruise-ship terminals on Honolulu Harbor – Pier 2 and Pier 11, by the Aloha Tower. Both are in downtown Honolulu and about 3 miles (5 km) from Waikīkī. Taxis and shuttles can take you to your hotel, and there's a car-rental company just a few blocks south of the piers, on Ala Moana Blvd.

Getting Around by Car

Unless you plan to stick to the Honolulu and Waikīkī area, it may be wise to rent a car so that you can see more of the island. Virtually every major national car-rental company is represented in Honolulu, such as **Advantage, Avis, Budget, Enterprise, Hertz,** and **National**. Car-rental companies in Waikīkī will have better rates.

Seat belts for everyone and approved car seats for children under three are mandatory, and pedestrians always have the right of way. Do not use your cell phone while driving, or you'll face a hefty fine. Keep the gas tank at least half-full – distances between gas stations may be long. Gas prices are much higher in Hawaii than on the US mainland.

Honolulu has its traffic challenges, especially when commuters come in and go out of town, but outside the city, driving is more relaxed. Locals will never sound their car horns except in a case of imminent danger, so check your rear-view mirror often to see if someone wants to pass you.

People in Hawaiʻi don't give directions in terms of east, west, north, and south. Instead, you will often hear the words ʻEwa (toward ʻEwa Beach), *mauka* (toward the mountains), and *makai* (toward the ocean).

Getting Around by Bus

You can get just about anywhere on Oʻahu by TheBus. You can purchase one-way tickets (exact cash is needed since no change is given) or a visitor's pass. The pass lets you ride all you want on any four consecutive days and is sold at **7-Eleven** stores and various other outlets and supermarkets. Convenience stores in Honolulu stock the bus map, which also has a handy guide to Honolulu attractions. A brand-new urban rail rapid transit system, the first of its kind in Hawaii, is set to open in late 2020. The first phase of this ambitious project will link East Kapolei to the Aloha Stadium. The second phase will continue the line into Honolulu.

Getting Around by Trolley

The open-air trolleys you'll see rolling around town, run by **Waikiki Trolley**, are a fun and cheap way to get around. The five routes cover Chinatown and the historic sites (red line), Pearl Harbor (purple line), Diamond Head (green line), ocean viewpoints (blue line), and shopping destinations (pink line). Tickets can be purchased on board, at tour desks, or through the website.

Getting Around by Taxi

For short, in-town trips you can get a taxi in front of any major hotel, and restaurants are happy to call a taxi for you after your meal. Many hotels also provide a shuttle service, usually to shopping destinations, sometimes to sights. Both taxis and shuttles are called in advance rather than hailed on the street. Rates are fixed, but pre-reserved round trips can be more economical.

Ride-sharing firms such as **Uber** and **Lyft** operate in O'ahu, mostly in Honolulu, although they cannot operate at the airport due to licensing restrictions. Other good taxi companies include **Charley's Taxi, Go808Express Shuttle, Roberts Hawaii Express Shuttle, Yellow Cab Honolulu Taxi, SpeediShuttle,** and **Hawaii23 Shuttle**.

Getting Around by Bicycle

Despite some dedicated bike lanes, O'ahu is not a bike-friendly island yet, though the city of Honolulu has plans to improve this in the future. Several outfitters offer downhill and mountain biking tours, such as **Bike Hawaii**. If you do decide to go out on your own, useful bike route maps are available from the **Hawaii Department of Transportation**.

DIRECTORY

ARRIVING BY AIR

Air Canada
🔲 aircanada.ca

Air New Zealand
🔲 airnewzealand.com

Alaska Airlines
🔲 alaskaair.com

American Airlines
🔲 aa.com

Honolulu International Airport (HNL)
🔲 hawaii.gov/hnl

Qantas
🔲 qantas.com

TheBus
🔲 thebus.org

WestJet
🔲 westjet.com

GETTING AROUND BY CAR

Advantage
🔲 advantage.com

Avis
🔲 avis.com

Budget
🔲 budget.com

Enterprise
🔲 enterprise.com

Hertz
🔲 hertz.com

National
🔲 nationalcar.com

GETTING AROUND BY BUS

7-Eleven
🔲 7elevenhawaii.com

GETTING AROUND BY TROLLEY

Waikiki Trolley
🔲 waikikitrolley.com

GETTING AROUND BY TAXI

Charley's Taxi
🔲 charleystaxi.com

Go808Express Shuttle
🔲 go808express.com

Hawaii23 Shuttle
🔲 hawaii23.com

Lyft
🔲 lyft.com

Roberts Hawaii Express Shuttle
🔲 robertshawaii.com

SpeediShuttle
🔲 speedishuttle.com

Uber
🔲 uber.com

Yellow Cab Honolulu Taxi
🔲 honolulu-taxi.com

GETTING AROUND BY BICYCLE

Bike Hawaii
🔲 bikehawaii.com

Hawaii Department of Transportation
🔲 hidot.hawaii.gov

Practical Information

Passports and Visas

Visitors from most European countries and from Australia, New Zealand, Chile, Japan, Singapore, and South Korea need a passport that is valid for at least six months from the date that they plan to enter O'ahu. They must also apply online for an **ESTA** (Electronic System for Travel Authorization) in advance of traveling to Hawaii. Canadians must show a valid passport. Other foreign nationals need a valid passport and a tourist visa, obtainable from a US consulate or embassy in their home country. Having proof of a return ticket is also strongly recommended.

Customs Regulations

Most meat, vegetables, fruit, and plants cannot be brought into O'ahu. This is meant to protect the island's unique environment, which is rather fragile due to its isolated geographical location. Any luggage leaving O'ahu is subject to an agricultural search, since only certain fruits and flowers may be taken out, such as pineapples and *leis*, so make sure you ask about this when you're purchasing such items.

Traditional Hawaiians believe that everything – every stone, every shell, every plant – has both a life and a place of its own. So feel free to look, enjoy, and touch natural objects, but refrain from removing anything from its home. Known as Pele's Curse, taking lava rocks off the island is especially *kapu* (forbidden) and is believed to bring bad luck.

Travel Safety Advice

Visitors can get up-to-date travel safety information from the **UK Foreign and Commonwealth Office**, the **US Department of State**, and the **Australian Department of Foreign Affairs and Trade**.

Travel Insurance

The cost of medical care is high everywhere in the US, including O'ahu, so travel insurance is highly recommended. If you have a mainland health insurance plan, you should check to see if it is accepted in Hawaii.

Health

As in the rest of the US, dialing 911 in O'ahu will put you in touch with the **Emergency Services**. There are several major medical centers in the city of Honolulu – **Queen's Medical Center**, **Kaiser Permanente**, **Straub Clinic and Hospital**, and the **Kapi'olani Medical Center**, to name just a few. There are clinics all over the island, too, and most resort hotels have doctors on call for their guests. **Longs Drugs** and **Walgreens** are good general pharmacies for prescriptions and over-the-counter medicines.

Tap water in O'ahu is perfectly safe to drink, but do not drink from or swim in streams, ponds, rivers, waterfalls, or freshwater pools since you may be running the risk of getting infected with leptospirosis, a bacterial disease that can be fatal if not treated in time.

Watch out for scorpions in the arid regions, and for centipedes and mosquitoes in the rainforests. Out in the water, the box jellyfish and Portuguese man-of-war can deliver painful stings, while coral and sea urchins can be quite sharp if accidentally stepped on, and can also cause infections in any resulting cuts that aren't cleaned properly.

Personal Security

Unfortunately, even in these paradise-like surroundings, theft can be a problem, and tourists' rental cars are often targeted. Always lock your car, even if you are leaving it for just a few moments. Never leave anything of value in view. Remember to make use of the safe in your hotel (or the lock boxes in rental properties) to store your jewelry, cash, and other valuables. Keep hotel and condo doors locked, including balcony doors.

Crime is not nearly the problem it is in some of the other major US cities, but Honolulu is a big place, and it has its share of less salubrious neighborhoods. Check with your hotel concierge about areas to avoid, especially late at night.

Travelers with Specific Needs

Oʻahu extends a warm aloha to travelers with specific needs. Due in large part to the Americans with Disabilities Act (ADA), hotels, restaurants, and attractions provide wheelchair ramps, designated parking places, and accessible restrooms. Braille translations of elevator button panels and other important signs are commonplace.

Currency and Banking

The currency in Oʻahu is the US dollar. Bring a mix of cash, credit cards, and travelers' checks with you – there are currency-exchange booths at the airport and in town. ATMs can be found in hotels, shopping centers, grocery stores, and outside most banks. **Bank of Hawaii** and **First Hawaiian Bank** are Oʻahu's largest, with locations throughout the island, including some inside supermarkets. In general, banks are open from 8:30am to 3 or 4pm Monday to Thursday, and from 8:30am to 6pm on Friday. Some branches are open on Saturdays.

VISA and **MasterCard** are universally accepted, except by the smallest stores and roadside stands. Most places also accept **Discover**, **Diners Club**, and **American Express**. US currency travelers' checks are widely accepted, but change will be given in cash. Lost or stolen travelers' checks are easily replaced.

Telephone and Internet

With only a few pay phones left in Oʻahu, you'll probably want to rely on your cell phone during your visit, since in-room hotel phones will have very high rates. Check with your cell-phone company about rates and travel packages that may include data plans for internet usage. It is also possible to purchase an inexpensive cell phone from Walmart or a SIM card from **AT&T**, **T-Mobile**, or **Hoku Wireless**.

To make calls to the other Hawaiian islands, the mainland, and to Canada, dial 1 followed by the area code and the seven-digit number. For other international calls, dial 011 followed by the country code, the city code, and the number you are calling.

Wi-Fi is readily available at most condos and hotels, and it is often included in the rate. Many cafés, shopping centers, and restaurants also offer complimentary Wi-Fi.

DIRECTORY

PASSPORTS AND VISAS

ESTA
w esta.cbp.dhs.gov

TRAVEL SAFETY ADVICE

Australian Department of Foreign Affairs and Trade
w dfat.gov.au
w smartraveller.gov.au

UK Foreign and Commonwealth Office
w gov.uk/foreign-travel-advice

US Department of State
w travel.state.gov

HEALTH

Emergency Services
c 911

Kaiser Permanente
w healthy.kaiserpermanente.org

Kapiʻolani Medical Center
w hawaiipacifichealth.org

Longs Drugs
w cvs.com

Queen's Medical Center
w queensmedicalcenter.net

Straub Clinic and Hospital
w hawaiipacifichealth.org

Walgreens
w walgreens.com

CURRENCY AND BANKING

American Express
w americanexpress.com

Bank of Hawaii
w boh.com

Diners Club
w dinersclub.com

Discover
w discover.com

First Hawaiian Bank
w fhb.com

MasterCard
w mastercard.com

VISA
w visa.com

TELEPHONE AND INTERNET

AT&T
w att.com

Hoku Wireless
w hokuwireless.com

T-Mobile
w t-mobile.com

Postal Services

Posting a letter in Oʻahu costs the same as on the US mainland, but mail sometimes takes longer to reach its destination. Hotels will often post mail for you, but otherwise there are post offices in every town. Opening hours are usually 8:30am to 4:30pm Monday to Friday, with short morning hours at some branches on Saturdays.

TV, Radio, and Newspapers

Oceanic Cable TV Channel 16 is a treasure trove of entertaining local information. Check it out, even if the pidgin (local slang) proves a little difficult to understand. All major hotels have their own visitor channels with programming providing an overview of the island, activities, shops, and restaurants. Fans of every music genre – from rock to country to Hawaiian – will find something on the radio dial to satisfy them. If you want to listen like the locals do, try **KINE** (105 FM) for the best in island sounds.

Hawaii's main daily newspaper, the **Honolulu Star-Advertiser**, covers all aspects of the news and is available at most hotels, grocery and convenience stores, cafés, gas stations, and online.

Opening Hours

Large shopping centers tend to open from 9am to 9pm Monday to Saturday; Sunday hours are usually shorter. Some supermarkets and convenience stores stay open 24 hours. Most retail stores are open on US holidays with the exception of Christmas Day, New Year's Day, and Hawaii state holidays, such as Prince Kūhiō Day (March 26) and King Kamehameha Day (June 11).

Time Difference

Unlike the US mainland, Hawaii does not subscribe to Daylight Savings Time – time across the islands remains constant throughout the year. From October to April, Hawaii is two hours behind the US West Coast (10 hours behind GMT); from April to October it is three hours behind the West Coast (11 hours behind GMT).

Electrical Appliances

Standard US current is 110–120 volts. Non-US appliances will need a converter as well as a plug adapter with two flat pins. Many hotels provide their guests with irons, coffee makers, and hair dryers in their rooms.

Weather

Contrary to popular belief, Hawaii does have seasons. Rain is common from October to January, and summer is much warmer than winter. Big surf arrives on the north shores in winter; south swells delight surfers in summer. At sea level, day temperatures average high 70s to mid-80s° F (25–31° C) most of the year; night temperatures can drop to the 60s° F (15–19° C), and sometimes even to the 50s° F (10–13° C) in winter.

During heavy rains, Oʻahu's streams and rivers are susceptible to flash floods, and although the many waterfalls on the island will be at their fullest, it is best not to venture out on hikes or unfamiliar drives during this time. Visitors should note that it is generally drier on the western or leeward side and wetter on the eastern or windward side of Oʻahu.

Visitor Information

The **Oʻahu Visitors Bureau** is the island's chapter of the Hawaii Visitors and Conventions Bureau (HVCB) and serves as the official source of information for visitors. Hawaiian Airlines' in-flight magazine **Hana Hou!** and the **Honolulu Magazine** are also great sources of information. All of these can be easily accessed online.

For updated online coverage of local news, videos, photo galleries, and event listings, visit websites such as **Hawaii Reporter** and **MidWeek**.

Books for suggested reading include James Michener's *Hawaii*, considered by many a must-read for visitors. It is certainly epic in scope and an entertaining, if not precisely accurate, historical novel. *Shoal of Time* by Gavan Daws, *Hawaii's Story by Hawaii's Queen* by Queen Liliuʻokalani, and *Hawaiian Mythology* by Martha Beckwith are all excellent choices, too.

Your hotel concierge is potentially one of the best

sources of local insider information. Concierges are, of course, residents of the island, and many know every nook and cranny of Oʻahu – where to get the best mai tai or that vintage piece of Hawaiiana you're after. Remember to tip them well if their advice is good.

Trips and Tours

By sea, by air, by land, even under the sea – every variety of guided tour is available on Oʻahu. Some tours to consider are **One Ocean** for an educational swimming-with-sharks experience, **Hawaii Food Tours** for adventurous foodies, and **Aloha Trikke** for electric three-wheel rides up Diamond Head and other areas of the island. See pages 46–7 and 52–3 for more tour and trek ideas.

Shopping

You'll save money on souvenirs, resort wear, and even groceries if you shop where the locals do. Local favorite **Longs Drugs** (see p113) has locations all over Oʻahu and is a great source for macadamia nuts and coffee, among other things. If you have a Costco card, you can purchase souvenirs in bulk there. Farmers' markets are another option for local items, and there's a big weekend swap meet at the Aloha Stadium for excellent buys on flowers, local produce, and crafts.

A 4.5 percent sales tax called "excise tax" is added onto everything you buy, including groceries,

retail goods, restaurant meals, accommodation, medicine, and services.

Dining

Oʻahu has a remarkable choice of restaurant options to suit all tastes and budgets. Local cuisine (in the form of plate lunches) is good value, and you'll find Vietnamese, Chinese, Japanese, Mexican, and Korean eateries all over the island, though the best bets are usually in Chinatown and Honolulu's suburbs. Food trucks are another inexpensive and delicious option.

Most restaurants cater to families and offer high chairs and *keiki* (child) menus. Only a few restaurants require guests to wear anything fancier than a shirt with a collar and decent footwear of some kind.

Restaurant tips should be at least 15 percent of the total amount, and 20 percent if the service was excellent. Reservations, if available, are recommended.

Accommodation

Hotel rooms in Oʻahu are generally quite expensive, especially those at the oceanfront resorts. You can expect to pay at least $250 per night to stay at a mid-range hotel and $200 per night at a hotel a block or two away from the beach. You will also need to factor in tax (a total of 13.75 percent for accommodations), possible resort fees (around $25 per day), and parking (around $20 per day). There are quite a lot

of options, however, for budget visitors, including renting a room in a house or a condo (try **Airbnb** or **VRBO**), or staying at a family-run B&B or a local inn. Another popular alternative for intrepid vacationers is camping under the stars via **Hawaii State Parks**.

Remember that during the low season (April to June and mid-September to late November), hotel and condo rates will be at their most reasonable.

DIRECTORY

TV, RADIO, AND NEWSPAPERS

Honolulu Star-Advertiser
w staradvertiser.com

KINE
w hawaiian105.com

VISITOR INFORMATION

Hana Hou!
w hanahou.com

Hawaii Reporter
w hawaiireporter.com

Honolulu Magazine
w honolulumagazine.com

MidWeek
w midweek.com

Oʻahu Visitors Bureau
w gohawaii.com

TRIPS AND TOURS

Aloha Trikke
w alohatrikke.com

Hawaii Food Tours
w hawaiifoodtours.com

One Ocean
w oneoceandiving.com

ACCOMMODATION

Airbnb
w airbnb.com

Hawaii State Parks
w hawaiistateparks.org

VRBO
w vrbo.com

Places to Stay

PRICE CATEGORIES
For a standard, double room per night (with breakfast if included), taxes, and extra charges.

$ under $200 $$ $200–400 $$$ over $400

Luxury Hotels

Aston Waikiki Sunset
MAP M7 ■ 229 Paoakalani Ave ■ 922 0511 ■ www.astonwaikikisunset.com ■ $$
Perfect for families, this high-rise condominium close to the beach and Honolulu Zoo features one- and two-bedroom suites with fully equipped kitchens. There's also a playground and a barbecue area.

Embassy Suites Waikiki Beach Walk
MAP K7 ■ 201 Beachwalk St ■ 921 2345 ■ www.embassysuiteswaikiki.com ■ $$
This all-suite hotel with impeccable amenities is ideal for families and groups. All guests enjoy spacious suites and a nightly poolside reception.

Hawaii Prince Hotel Waikiki
MAP G6 ■ 100 Holomoana St ■ 956 1111 ■ www.princeresortshawaii.com ■ $$
Each of the rooms at this marina-front hotel overlooks the picturesque Ala Wai Yacht Harbor. There are two award-winning restaurants: 100 Sails offers Hawaiian cuisine, and Katsumidoro Tokyo has excellent sushi. The hotel is very close to the Ala Moana Shopping Center, Waikīkī nightlife, and downtown Honolulu.

Hilton Hawaiian Village
MAP H6 ■ 2005 Kālia Rd ■ 949 4321 ■ www.hiltonhawaiianvillage.com ■ $$
Set on the widest stretch of popular Waikīkī Beach, this huge hotel has six towers, five pools, more than 90 shops, 20 lounges and restaurants, a spa, and tropical gardens.

Hyatt Regency Waikiki Resort & Spa
MAP L7 ■ 2424 Kalākaua Ave ■ 923 1234 ■ www.hyatt.com ■ $$
An atrium with a cascading waterfall joins the two 40-story towers of this impressive Waikīkī resort. The seafood restaurant features open-air seating with ocean views.

The Modern Honolulu
MAP G6 ■ 1775 Ala Moana Blvd ■ 943 5800 ■ www.themodernhonolulu.com ■ $$
In addition to stylish rooms, guests at this trendy resort enjoy a sunrise pool and a sunset beach. Iron Chef Morimoto's restaurant is a worthy in-house dining destination.

Outrigger Reef on the Beach
MAP J7 ■ 2169 Kālia Rd ■ 923 3111 ■ www.outriggerreef-onthebeach.com ■ $$
Right on the beach near Fort DeRussy, this hotel's highlights include a pool, the oceanside La'akea Spa (see p56), and nightly Hawaiian entertainment. It is also known for its Hawaiian-themed wedding vow renewal ceremonies.

Royal Hawaiian Hotel
MAP K7 ■ 2259 Kalākaua Ave ■ 923 7311 ■ www.royal-hawaiian.com ■ $$
Everything at the "Pink Palace of the Pacific," a Waikīkī landmark since 1927, is pink – from the stucco exterior to the towels. Its Royal Beach Tower is pricier, but many would say the Historic Wing has more charm.

Sheraton Moana Surfrider
MAP K7 ■ 2365 Kalākaua Ave ■ 922 3111 ■ www.moana-surfrider.com ■ $$
Hawaiian details combine with modern comfort here. Contemporary Hawaiian entertainment in the Beach Bar is a highlight of any visit.

Sheraton Waikiki
MAP K7 ■ 2255 Kalākaua Ave ■ 922 4422 ■ www.sheraton-waikiki.com ■ $$
This sleek 1,700-room hotel towers over the beach at Waikīkī – most rooms have spectacular ocean views. You can admire Waikīkī's sparkling lights from the infinity pool bar and grill.

Turtle Bay Resort
MAP C1 ■ 57–091 Kamehameha Hwy, Kahuku ■ 293 6000 ■ www.turtlebayresort.com ■ $$
On a stretch of oceanfront on the North Shore, this

resort has rooms, beach cottages, and ocean villas. There are plenty of sports activities, and the on-site Spa Luana offers a wide range of services.

Four Seasons Resort Oahu at Ko Olina
MAP D5 ▪ 92 1001 Olani St, Kapolei ▪ 679 0079 ▪ www.fourseasons.com ▪ $$$
With pools, tennis courts, golf, a cultural center, kids' activities, and top-notch restaurants, this is a plush five-star beach resort. Some suites have private gardens with plunge pools.

Halekulani
MAP J7 ▪ 2199 Kālia Rd ▪ 923 2311 ▪ www.halekulani.com ▪ $$$
This hotel on the beach has manicured tropical grounds, tasteful decor, a spa, superb cuisine at La Mer (see p81), and its signature "orchid pool."

Kahala Hotel & Resort
MAP E6 ▪ 5000 Kāhala Ave ▪ 739 8888 ▪ www.kahalaresort.com ▪ $$$
On a great swimming beach and close to plenty of golf, this resort is known for its lagoon, where guests can mix with bottlenose dolphins through the Dolphin Encounters program.

Marriott Ko Olina Beach Club
MAP B5 ▪ 92-161 Waipahe Pl, Kapolei ▪ 679 4700 ▪ www.marriott.com ▪ $$$
Stay in large, comfortable beachfront condos with high-end appliances, balconies, and several pools. The man-made lagoons of Ko Olina are ideal for kids to swim in.

The Ritz-Carlton Residences, Waikīkī Beach
MAP J5 ▪ 383 Kalaimoku St ▪ 922 8111 ▪ www.ritzcarlton.com ▪ $$$
Just a short walk from the beach, this establishment has ocean views from every spacious room, plus kitchenettes, complimentary Wi-Fi, and a 24-hour gym. The infinity pool is surrounded by private cabanas.

Mid-Price Hotels

Park Shore
MAP M7 ▪ 2586 Kalākaua Ave ▪ 923 0411 ▪ www.parkshorewaikiki.com ▪ $
Located across from Kapi'olani Park, at the Diamond Head end of Waikīkī, just steps from the beach, this hotel offers a premium location without premium prices. Rooms are comfortable, and there's a 24-hour family restaurant on site.

Shoreline Hotel Waikīkī
MAP K6 ▪ 342 Seaside Ave ▪ 931 2444 ▪ www.jdvhotels.com ▪ $
This modern boutique hotel uses sleek, minimalist decor and natural motifs to evoke classic Hawaiian serenity. It is just steps from the beach and exclusive shopping options. The rooftop pool provides an optional escape from beach crowds.

Vive Hotel Waikīkī
MAP K6 ▪ 2426 Kūhiō Ave ▪ 687 2000 ▪ www.vivehotelwaikiki.com ▪ $
The Vive is located a few blocks from the beach. Although the modern rooms are on the smaller side, they are great value. The hotel offers beach gear hire, and is close to shops and restaurants.

Waikiki Gateway Hotel
MAP J5 ▪ 2070 Kalākaua Ave ▪ 955 3741 ▪ www.waikikigateway.com ▪ $
On the corner of two main streets at the north end of Waikīkī, this high-rise has a range of rooms to suit most budgets, and a pleasant pool.

'Alohilani Resort
MAP L7 ▪ 2490 Kalākaua Ave ▪ 922 1233 ▪ www.pacificbeachhotel.com ▪ $$
In the middle of Waikīkī, this hotel is centered around a three-story-tall aquarium. Other features include a tennis court, pool and whirlpool, salon and spa, and lobby shops.

Aqua Oasis
MAP K6 ▪ 320 Lewers St ▪ 923 2300 ▪ www.aquaoasishotel.com ▪ $$
This boutique hotel off the main drag is a hidden treasure. One of the two towers has suites, while the other has regular rooms. Perks include a pool and sundeck and a shuttle to the Ala Moana Shopping Center.

Diamond Head Beach Hotel
MAP E6 ▪ 2947 Kalākaua Ave ▪ 922 1928 ▪ www.obrhi.com ▪ $$
The serene oceanfront setting at the base of Diamond Head, away from the bustle of Waikīkī, makes up for the simplicity of these condos just a short walk from Kalākaua Avenue's dining and shopping scenes.

Hilton Waikiki Beach

MAP M6 ▪ 2500 Kūhiō Ave ▪ 922 0811 ▪ www.hilton.com ▪ $$

A short walk to Kūhiō Beach, this hotel has an American restaurant and several bars, as well as a 10th-floor pool deck.

Holiday Inn Waikiki Beachcomber

MAP K6 ▪ 2300 Kalākaua Ave ▪ 922 4646 ▪ www.waikikibeachcomber resort.com ▪ $$

Across the street from Waikīkī Beach and near the Royal Hawaiian Shopping Center, this hotel has a 400-seat buffet and hosts the Magic of Polynesia show.

'Ilima Hotel

MAP K6 ▪ 445 Nohonani St ▪ 923 1877 ▪ www.ilima.com ▪ $$

All the one-, two-, and three-bedroom suites and the studios are spacious, with kitchens. Local calls are included in the rates, and there is free Wi-Fi. There's also a pool, exercise room, and sauna.

Lotus Honolulu at Diamond Head

MAP L7 ▪ 2885 Kalākaua Ave ▪ 922 1700 ▪ www.lotushonoluluhotel.com ▪ $$

This chic boutique hotel with a Zen vibe is just a short stroll from the beach. It offers ocean and mountains views, in-room coffee makers, and bike and beach gear rentals.

New Otani Kaimana Beach Hotel

MAP M7 ▪ 2863 Kalākaua Ave ▪ 923 1555 ▪ www.kaimana.com ▪ $$

Rooms at this boutique hotel are small, but the Sans Souci Beach location, opposite Kapi'olani Park, with easy access to the Honolulu Zoo and the Waikīkī Shell, more than makes up for it. The beachside Hau Tree Lanai restaurant has the best *poi* waffles in town.

Outrigger Waikiki Beach Resort

MAP K7 ▪ 2335 Kalākaua Ave ▪ 923 0711 ▪ www.outrigger.com ▪ $$

The 500 rooms at this oceanfront hotel, the jewel in the crown of the Outrigger chain, feature Polynesian decor. The popular beachfront Duke's Waikiki restaurant often hosts contemporary Hawaiian entertainers.

Sheraton Princess Ka'iulani

MAP L6 ▪ 120 Ka'iulani Ave ▪ 922 5811 ▪ www.princess-kaiulani.com ▪ $$

This hotel offers all the advantages of a Sheraton hotel without the ocean-front prices. It is home to a revue (*Creation – A Polynesian Journey*), an all-you-can-eat buffet restaurant, and a Japanese restaurant.

Surfjack Hotel & Swim Club

MAP K5 ▪ 412 Lewers St ▪ 923 8882 ▪ www.surfjack.com ▪ $$

In a quiet area away from the beachfront, this boutique hotel has vintage decor and works of art by local artists. Enjoy poolside cocktails and a range of *pūpū* (appetizers) from the superb Mahina & Sun's restaurant (*see p81*), or borrow the hotel's free bikes for a ride around town.

Waikiki Shore

MAP J7 ▪ 2161 Kālia Rd ▪ 952 4500 ▪ www.castleresorts.com ▪ $$

Most of the one- and two-bed suites and studios at this oceanfront condo complex in Waikīkī feature breathtaking views, especially those on the upper floors. All units have a kitchen and laundry facilities.

Budget Hotels

Kailua Beach Properties

MAP F4 ▪ 204 S. Kalaheo Ave, Kailua ▪ 261 1653 ▪ www.patskailua.com ▪ $–$$$

Groups of friends or families who would like to experience Hawaii like locals would do well to consider staying at one of these fully furnished homes and cottages in beautiful residential areas of Kailua and Lanikai, on O'ahu's windward side.

Ke 'Iki Beach Bungalows

MAP B1 ▪ 59–579 Ke'Iki Rd, Hale'iwa ▪ 638 8829 ▪ www.keikibeach.com ▪ $

These modest yet clean, comfortable beach cottages occupy their own stretch of sand between the surfing beaches of Waimea Bay and Banzai Pipeline. Run by a local resident, they offer family-style accommodation.

Pagoda Hotel

MAP B6 ▪ 1525 Rycroft St ▪ 941 6611 ▪ www.pagodahotel.com ▪ $

Popular with locals thanks to its proximity to the shops at Ala Moana, this hotel offers a variety of rooms – standard, studios with kitchenettes, and suites. The floating restaurant and water gardens are lovely.

Ramada Plaza Waikiki

MAP H6 ▪ 1830 Ala Moana Blvd ▪ 955 1111 ▪ www.ramada.com ▪ $
This 17-story high-rise hotel is at the gateway to Waikīkī and just two blocks from the beach. There's a pool with sun-deck, and a fitness facility. A Chinese buffet restaurant offers affordable, bountiful Asian fare.

Royal Grove Hotel

MAP L6 ▪ 151 Uluniu Ave ▪ 923 7691 ▪ www.royalgrovehotel.com ▪ $
This pink, family-run hotel in a convenient central location oozes retro character. Ask for a room with air-conditioning, since not all rooms have it. Beach gear is free to use, and there is a lively pool area.

White Sands Hotel

MAP K6 ▪ 431 Nohonani St ▪ 924 7263 ▪ www.whitesandshotel.com ▪ $
Most guest rooms at this basic hotel two blocks from the beach are fitted with kitchenettes. There is a pool, coin laundry room, and parking on site. Pet-friendly rooms are available.

Inns and B&Bs

Hawaii's Hidden Hideaway B&B

MAP F4 ▪ 1369 Mokulua Dr, Kailua ▪ 877 443 3299 ▪ www.ahawaiibnb.com ▪ $
One of the island's top-rated B&Bs, this

establishment offers private entrances, bathtubs, and kitchen/dining areas, as well as complimentary beach items, a laundry, *lanai*, and excellent breakfasts. The building is well located right across from the beach.

Hula Breeze

MAP F4 ▪ 172 Kuumele Pl, Kailua ▪ 469 7623 ▪ $
Surrounded by tropical gardens, these private cottages located near Kailua beach provide the perfect accommodation for a romantic getaway. They offer spacious, clean, comfortable rooms, each of which comes with a kitchenette.

Kalani Hawaii

MAP B2 ▪ 59–222 B. Kamahameha Hwy, Haleʻiwa ▪ 781 6415 ▪ www.kalanihawaii.com ▪ $
Located amid luscious green vegetation and expansive stretches of sand, Kalani Hawaii gives guests the opportunity to enjoy the island at its best. Choose from a range of rooms, houses, and studios in this North Shore resort.

Manoa Valley Inn

MAP C6 ▪ 2001 Vancouver Dr ▪ 947 6019 ▪ www.manoavalleyinn.com ▪ $
This Victorian-style inn is located near the Univesity of Hawaii. Seven rooms and a single cottage provide guests with a quiet retreat from Honolulu's lights and action. Built in 1912, the Manoa Valley Inn is listed on the National Register of Historic Places.

Manu Mele Bed and Breakfast

MAP F4 ▪ 153 Kailuana Pl, Kailua ▪ 262 0016 ▪ www.manumele.net ▪ $
In a quiet suburban area near the beach, three comfortable suites with private entrances offer cooking facilities, air-conditioning and complimentary Wi-Fi. The gardens and pool are an added bonus.

Papaya Paradise B&B

MAP F4 ▪ 395 Auwinala Rd, Kailua ▪ 261 0316 ▪ www.windward-oahu.com ▪ $
Friendly hosts offer two private units about half a mile (1 km) from the beach, in the residential section of Kailua. Great value for money, this place offers a backyard pool and shared kitchen.

Pillows in Paradise Bed & Breakfast

MAP F4 ▪ 336 Awakea Rd, Kailua ▪ 262 8540 ▪ www.pillowsinparadise.com ▪ $
Two studio suites have private entrances, private bathrooms, kitchenettes, air-conditioning, complimentary Wi-Fi, and free parking. The beach is a ten-minute walk away, and a basket of fresh fruit and pastries welcomes you on your first morning.

Rainbow Inn

MAP D4 ▪ 98-1049 Mahola Pl, Aiea ▪ 486 3876 ▪ $
With its panoramic view of Pearl Harbor and large rooms, Rainbow Inn is great value for money. Its secluded location – as well as the ocean and mountains nearby and the friendly, helpful hosts – add to its charm.

For a key to hotel price categories see p116

Index

Acknowledgments

Author

Bonnie Friedman is a freelance writer and publicist living in Hawaii.

Additional contributor
Lisa Voormeij

Publishing Director Georgina Dee

Publisher Vivien Antwi

Design Director Phil Ormerod

Editorial Ankita Awasthi Tröger, Rachel Fox, Maresa Manara, Alison McGill, Rada Radojicic, Sally Schafer, Sands Publishing Solutions, Jackie Staddon, Hollie Teague

Design Tessa Bindloss, Bharti Karakoti

Cover Design Richard Czapnik

Commissioned Photography Rough Guides / Greg Ward

Picture Research Taiyaba Khatoon, Sumita Khatwani, Ellen Root

Cartography Uma Bhattacharya, Swati Handoo, Suresh Kumar, Casper Morris, Alok Pathak

DTP Jason Little

Production Poppy Werder-Harris

Factchecker Carolyn Patten

Proofreader Laura Walker

Indexer Hilary Bird

First edition created by Blue Island Publishing

Picture Credits

123RF.com: fominayaphoto 46t; globalphoto 104–5; Joshua Rainey 87cr; sorincolac 4b; Svitlana Tereshchenko 58cl.

4Corners: Susanne Kremer 3tl, 66–7; SIME / Giovanni Simeone 88–9.

Alamy Stock Photo: James Au 63br; Tibor Bognar 22cl; DanitaDelimont.com/ Charles Crust 62tl, / Michael DeFreitas 31bl; Design Pics Inc 77br, 97b; Douglas Peebles Photography 79bl, 90c, 94tl; dpa picture alliance 102c; Robert Fried 32cla, 32br; Stephen Goodwin 78–9; Jeff Greenberg 40cl; Kelly Headrick 72cla; Andre Jenny 103bl; Terry Kelly 82cl; Keith Levit 50-51; Angus McComiskey 98cla; Jon Mclean 45br; Leigh Anne Meeks 75cr; John De Mello 96cla; David L. Moore – Hawaii 14cl, 14–15, 38c; Photo Resource Hawaii 15c, 15br, 19c, 27cl, 57tr, 83t, 91tl, 100b; PJF Military Collection 65cl; Franco Salmoiraghi 55cl; Rob Smith 39cl; SOTK2011 41c; David Wall 86br; Andrew Woodley 70cl.

AWL Images: Danita Delimont Stock 42tl; Michele Falzone 4cl; Nordic Photos 1, 49tl.

Dreamstime.com: Adeliepenguin 16bl; Tomas Del Amo 50tl; Aquamarine4 29tl, 63cl; Bennymarty 13bl, 50cr, 76c; Boreccy 30bl; Boykov 32–3; James Crawford 19tl; Demerzel21 30–31; Eric Broder Van Dyke 4crb, 10clb, 73tl, 74bl, 77ca, 106tl; Eddygaleotti 11crb, 28–9; Edwardstewartii 41tl; Gordon Fahey 28cla; Joel Ferrer 13crb; Yun Gao 103tr; Gilles Gaonach 43cl; Jose Gil 11br; Izanbar 31tl; Jerryway 46clb; Andrii Kucher 95cl; Kungverylucky 59c; Ldionisio 62b; Rico Leffanta 23tl, 64bl; Viktoria Lelis 39tr; Chee-onn Leong 17br, 104clb; Mazikab 45c; Leigh Anne Meeks 43br, 48b, 91br, 105bl; Mkojot 54tr, 93cl, 99tl; MNStudio 4t, 98–9; Shane Myers 2tr, 11cl, 34–5, 84cla; Glenn Nagel 17tl, 18–19, 64t; NatashaBreen 101cra; Mihaela Nica 4clb; Photoblueice 33crb; Picturemakersllc 12–13; Marek Poplawski 36c; Ppy2010ha 58br; RightFramePhotoVideo 26–7; Daniel Shumny 29cr; Svetik48 61tr; Vacclav 10cla; Vasen 19br; Gerald Watanabe 27cb, 44bl, 45t, 84c; Ashley Werter 23br; Jeff Whyte 2tl, 8–9, 11cra, 16–17, 27tl, 68tr, 71cla, 78cl, 97cra.

Duke's Waikiki: 80t.

Getty Images: Rita Ariyoshi 59tl; Bill Bachmann 52br, 53cr; Ann Cecil 54b, 59br; Linda Ching 14br; David Inc 73crb; Design Pics / Ron Dahlquist 41br; Peter French 52t; Interim Archives 37cl; Lonely Planet Images 47bl; Cory Lum 65br; MCT 37br; MyLoupe 12crb; Douglas Peebles 70b; Sri Maiava Rusden 61cl; Brandon Tabiolo 38b; Universal History Archive 36bl.

Honolulu Museum of Art: 11tr, 24br, 24–5, 25tl, 25c, 25br.

Hotel Halekulani: 56tl, 81bl.

Iolani Palace: The Friends of Iolani Palace 10br, 18cla, 18br.

iStockphoto.com: BackyardProduction 3tr, 108–9; CampPhoto 49crb; compassandcamera 4cr; jewhyte 6br; KarenMassier 69tr; Kirkikis 20–21; LanaCanada 16clb, 68cl, 92br; littlestocker 72b; nantela 83br; PB57photos 42b; tropicalpixsingapore 4cla; Kenneth Wiedemann 22cra, 92t.

Koko Head Cafe: 60t.

Plumeria Beach House: The Kahala Hotel & Resort 107br.

Rainbow Watersports: 55tr.

Robert Harding Picture Library: Michael DeFreitas 84–5; North Light Images 7br; Douglas Peebles 10bl; Greg Vaughn 40br.

Royal Hawaiian Hotel: 26cl.

Sansei Seafood Restaurant & Sushi Bar: 60bl.

Sunset Yoga Hawai'i: Charlotte Davenport 57bl.

SuperStock: Prisma / Heeb Christian 85cl.

Cover

Front and spine: Getty Images: Brandon Tabiolo

Back: Dreamstime.com: Tomas Del Amo

Pull Out Map Cover

Getty Images: Brandon Tabiolo

All other images © Dorling Kindersley
For further information see:
www.dkimages.com

Penguin
Random
House

Printed and bound in China

First American Edition, 2004
Published in the United States by
DK Publishing, 345 Hudson Street,
New York, New York 10014

Copyright 2004, 2018 © Dorling
Kindersley Limited

A Penguin Random House Company

18 19 20 21 10 9 8 7 6 5 4 3 2 1

**Reprinted with revisions 2006, 2008,
2010, 2012, 2014, 2018**

Published in Great Britain by Dorling
Kindersley Limited.

A catalog record for this book is available
from the Library of Congress.

ISSN 1479-344X

ISBN 978 1 4654 6881 9

MIX
Paper from
responsible sources
FSC™ C018179

SPECIAL EDITIONS OF DK TRAVEL GUIDES

DK Travel Guides can be purchased
in bulk quantities at discounted prices
for use in promotions or as premiums.
We are also able to offer special
editions and personalized jackets,
corporate imprints, and excerpts from
all of our books, tailored specifically to
meet your own needs.

To find out more, please contact:

in the US
specialsales@dk.com

in the UK
travelguides@uk.dk.com

in Canada
specialmarkets@dk.com

in Australia
**penguincorporatesales@
penguinrandomhouse.com.au**

*As a guide to abbreviations in visitor information
blocks:* **Adm** = admission charge

Glossary of Useful Words and Terms

Hawaiian began as an oral language and was put into written form by missionaries who arrived in the 1820s. The teaching and speaking of Hawaiian was banned from the early 1900s, and by the time the native cultural renaissance began in 1978 the melodious language was almost totally lost. Immersion programs are beginning to produce a new generation of Hawaiian speakers, however, and you will hear Hawaiian words sprinkled in conversation and in the islands' music, as well as seeing it written on some signs.

Summary of Pronunciation
The Hawaiian language has just 12 letters: the five vowels plus h, k, l, m, n, p, and w.

unstressed vowels:
a = as in "*above*"
e = as in "*bet*"
i = as y in "*city*"
o = as in "*sole*"
u = as in "*full*"

stressed vowels:
ā = as in "*far*"
ē = as in "*pay*"
ī = as in "*see*"
ō = as in "*sole*"
ū = as in "*moon*"

consonants:
h = as in "*h*at"
k = as in "*k*ick"
l = as in "*l*aw"
m = as in "*m*ow"
n = as in "*n*ow"
p = as in "*p*in"
w = as in "*w*in" or "*v*ine"

The 'okina (glottal stop) is found at the beginning of some words beginning with vowels or between vowels. It is pronounced like the sound between the syllables in the English "uh-oh."

ali'i = ahlee-ee
liliko'i = leeleekoh-ee
'oha*na* = oh-hahnah

The kahakō (macron) is a mark found only above vowels, indicating vowels should be stressed.

kāne = kah-**nay**
kōkua = koh-**koo**-ah
pūpū = **poo**-poo

Everyday Words

aloha	ah-loh-ha	hello; goodbye; love
hale	ha-leh	house
hula	who-la	Hawaiian dance
kāhiko	**kaa**-hee-koh	old, traditional
kapa	kah-pah	bark cloth
keiki	kay-kee	child
kōkua	koh-koo-ah	help
lānai	luh-nigh	porch; balcony
lei	layh	garland
lua	looah	bathroom
mahalo	muh-ha-low	thank you
'ono	oh-noh	delicious
ko'olau	koh-oh-lowh	windward side

Geographical and Nature Terms

'a'ā	ah-aah	rough, jagged lava
kai	kaee	ocean
koholā	koh-hoh-**laah**	humpback whale
mauna	mau-nah	mountain
pāhoehoe	**pah**-hoy-hoy	smooth lava
pali	pah-lee	cliff
pu'u	poo-oo	hill
wai	w(v)hy	fresh water

Historical Terms

ali'i	ahlee-ee	chief; royalty
heiau	hey-yow	ancient temple
kahuna	kah-hoo-nah	priest; expert
kapu	kah-poo	taboo
kupuna	koo-poo-nah	elders; ancestors
luakini	looh-ah-kee-nee	human sacrifice temple
mana	mah-nah	supernatural power
mele	meh-leh	song
oli	oh-leeh	chant

Food Words

'ahi	ah-hee	yellowfin tuna
aku	ah-koo	skipjack; bonito
a'u	ah-oo	swordfish; marlin
haupia	how-peeah	coconut pudding
kalo	kah-loh	taro
kālua	**kah**-looah	food baked slowly in an underground oven
laulau	lau-lau	steamed filled ti-leaf packages
liliko'i	lee-lee-koh-ee	passion fruit
limu	lee-moo	seaweed
lomi-lomi salmon	low-me low-me	raw salmon with onion and tomato
lū'au	**loo**-ow	Hawaiian feast
mahimahi	muh-hee-muh-hee	dorado; dolphin fish
poi	poy	pounded taro
pūpū	**poo**-poo	appetizer
uku	oo-koo	gray snapper
ulua	oo-looah	jackfish

Pidgin

Hawaii's unofficial conglomerate language is commonly heard on the street and in backyards throughout Hawaii. You may hear:

brah	brother, pal
broke da mout'	great food
fo' real	really
fo' what	why
grinds	food; also to grind
howzit?	how's everything?
kay den	okay then
laydahs	later; goodbye
no can	cannot
no mo' nahting	nothing
shoots!	yeah!
stink eye	dirty look
talk story	chat; gossip